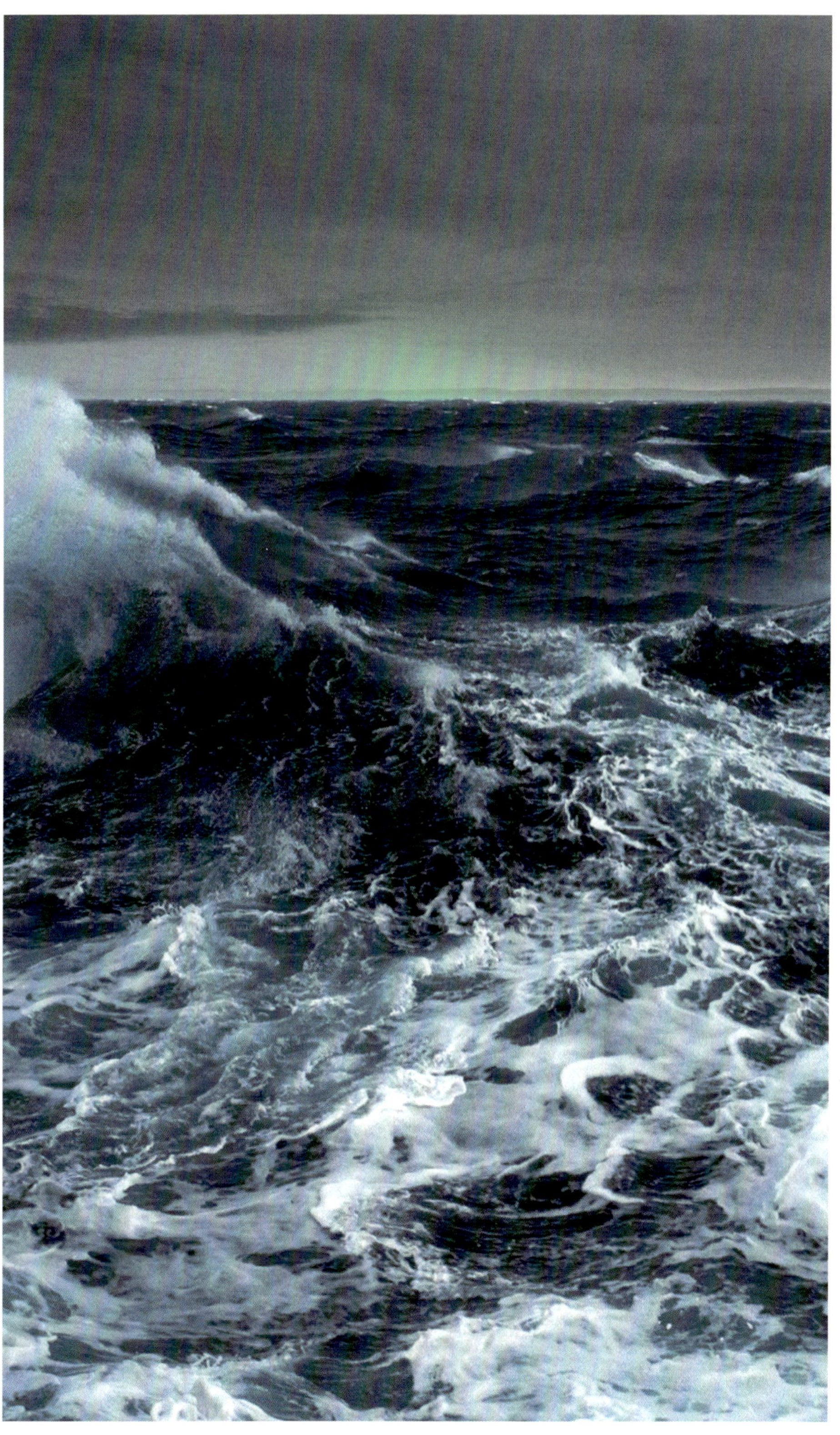

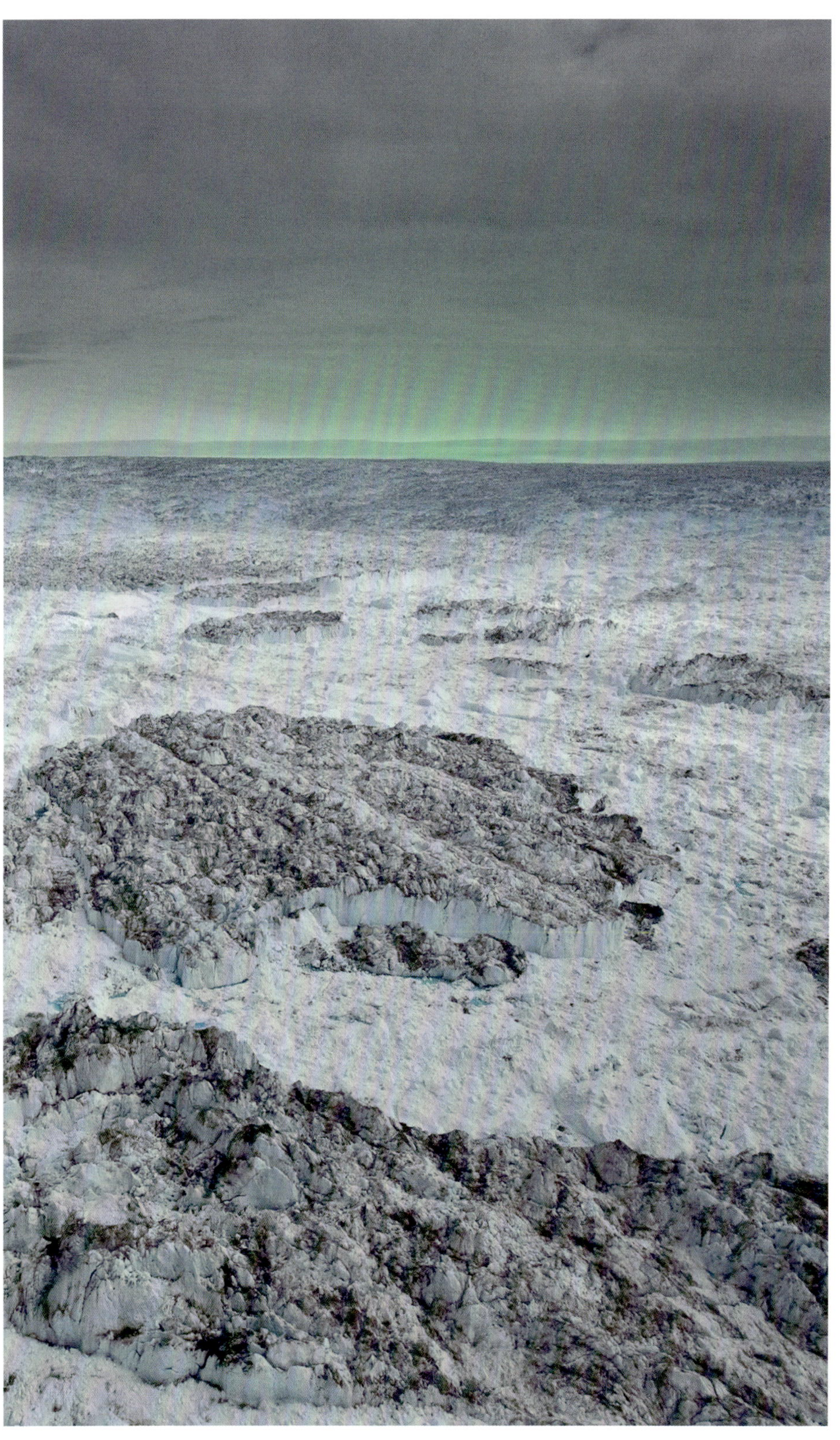

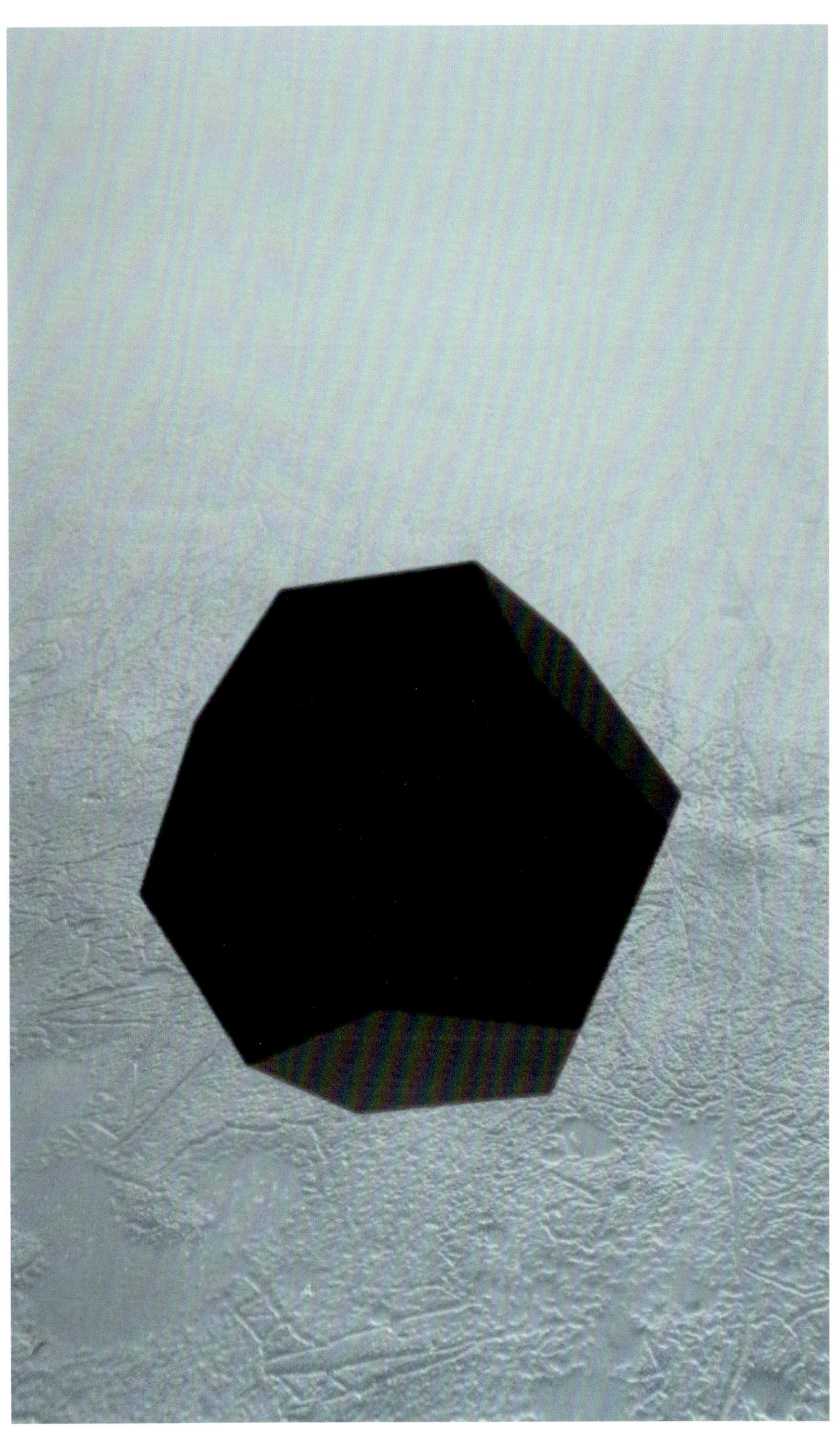

OBITUARY

SHAHRYAR NASHAT

with
SARAH LEHRER-GRAIWER

and
ANDREA FARAGUNA
AUDE LEHMANN

Sternberg Press

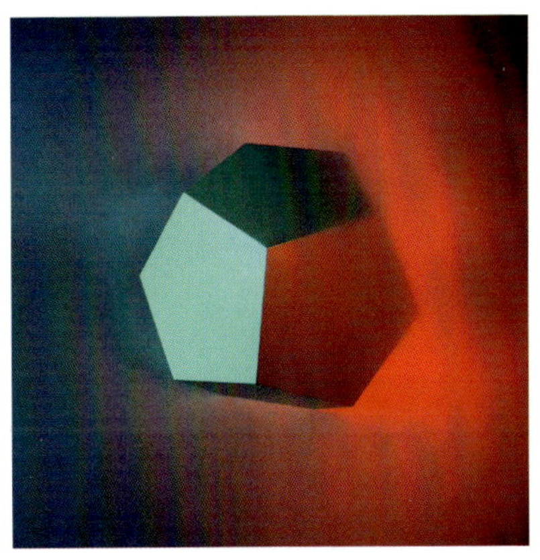

LA SHAPE,
A MODEL
DODECAHEDRON,
IS NO MORE

La Shape—diva prop, cult sculpture, model, performer, and muse who featured in numerous video works and photographs by Swiss artist Shahryar Nashat—passed away on August 29, 2014. It was nearly four years old and resided in Berlin.

The immediate circumstances of its passing suggest foul play. And yet, the thing's personal development, chronic psychosis, and shifting sense of self set the stage for what ultimately transpired. No forensic review was ordered, according to Nashat, the thing's guardian, creator, enabler, and number-one champion.

Admired as a fetish object by adventurous Platonists, animists, and speculative realists in cultural fields ranging from dance and film to philosophy and parlor magic, La Shape registered its biggest impact in the world of contemporary art. It emerged on the scene as part of a rather glam posse of shape-shifting, touch-sensitive, ultraphotogenic geo-metric bodies on the frontlines of the widely repressed Thing Rights & Object Solidarity movement. La Shape has been credited with advancing a burgeoning sociopolitical awareness of mindful things. Within its cohort of related rational shapes, it was the most pioneering and visible—something of a minor celebrity. Possessing a flawless figure and slanted silhouette, La Shape was known for its distinctive chroma-key-green pigmentation and dodecahedral structure faceted with congruent pentagonal sides.

While the other Platonic solids were said to carry an ancient mystical connection to the four elements of nature—cube/earth, tetrahedron/fire, octahedron/air, and icosahedron/water—the dodecahedron was extra special and abstract, associated by Plato (as well as certain modern-day cosmologists) with the structure of the universe itself, symbolizing the ethereal stuff of cosmic matter. In so many senses, La Shape was a true model. Its scale was mutable; whatever its size, it always conveyed the potential to be much bigger, or much smaller.

A geometric body with twelve faces, La Shape fused dance, film, theater, and portraiture to achieve strange new visual effects. La Shape's look stylishly combined a range of futurist, space-age-modern, digital, low-tech, and ancient formal tropes. During its brief but momentous existence, La Shape proved the potent agency, complex intelligence, and secretive life force of objects. Despite its green-screen coloring—with all the technological capabilities of projection and visual transformation implied therein—it refused to be keyed or swapped out for anything or anyone else. This refusal was delivered with an attitude of defiance and teenage rebellion, an act simultaneously of monkish asceticism and flagrant narcissism. As it once memorably stated, "Self-realization is as much a matter of sacrifice and negation as it is a matter of affirmative expression; it's as much a challenge of saying no and defining limits as it is about expansiveness and inclusive possibility." Posing as a chameleonic appropriator par excellence who would rather not appropriate—a technology on strike—intransigence and difficulty were at the very core of its objecthood. It studied well that golden rule of showbiz: keep your audience wanting more.

Claiming ambiguous gender and having prevaricated about its age and provenance in numerous interviews, La Shape's biography is suspect and mysterious by design. What we know is limited mostly to matters of public record, such as its corpus of still and moving pictures. One aspect of its character is absolutely clear and tellingly emblematic of a typical, twenty-first-century condition: it lived to be pictured and existed to be mediated.

La Shape was conceived on October 21, 2010, when it first occurred to its producer as an idea. The thought came to Shahryar Nashat while the artist was in Venice on a site visit to the Arsenale, where he was to exhibit the following year in the 54th Venice Biennale. Nashat, then 35, was based in Berlin and mounting exhibitions throughout Europe at the time. Employing video, photography, digital printing, and sculpture, his work is often characterized by an aesthetic of austere, toned desire and an interest in staging, rehearsal, museological modes of display, prop-like objects, and the interrupted, or cropped,

body. Nashat's lineage is sculptural and cinematic, photographic and theatrical; his images have a wry formality that may bring to mind the work of artists like Jack Goldstein, Stephen Prina, Hilary Lloyd, Mark Leckey, or Nairy Baghramian.

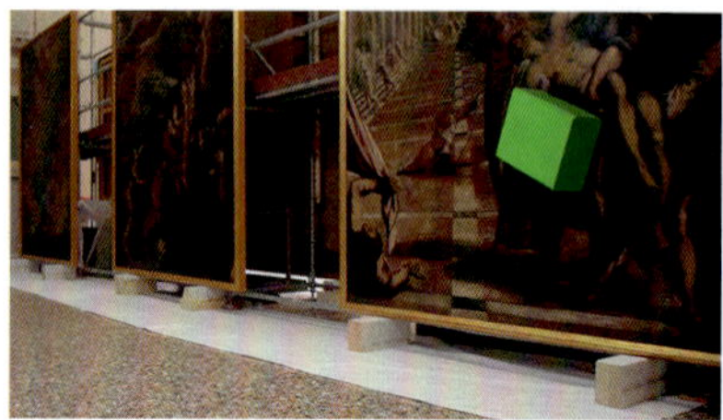

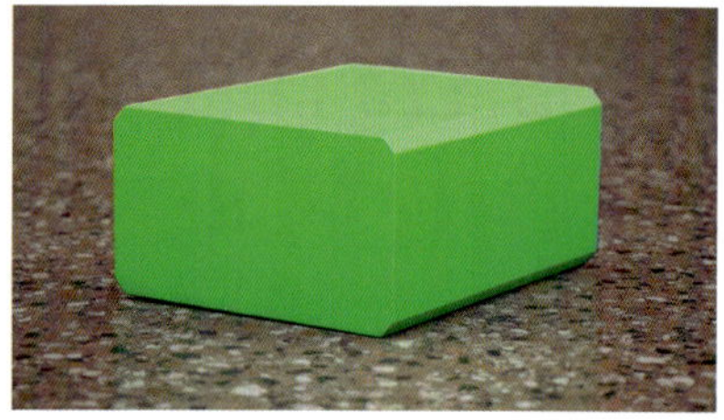

Stills of *Factor Green*, 2011

Developing from concept to product, La Shape entered the world a few months later as a sculptural volume, in early 2011. It was conceived specifically as a prop for Nashat's video *Factor Green*, in which its basic geometry serves as a stark, minimalist counterpoint to the many lavish and dramatic Tintoretto paintings in Venice's Gallerie dell'Accademia, where the movie is set. To that end, La Shape appeared on camera, luggage-sized, for the first time on May 1, 2011. This virginal encounter with the camera was formative and indelible, galvanizing La Shape's budding desire in tight relation to the lens. In fact, somewhat paradoxically, it was that first experience of being filmed, precisely positioned as an object to be looked at and acted upon, which awakened its internal subjectivity and sense of

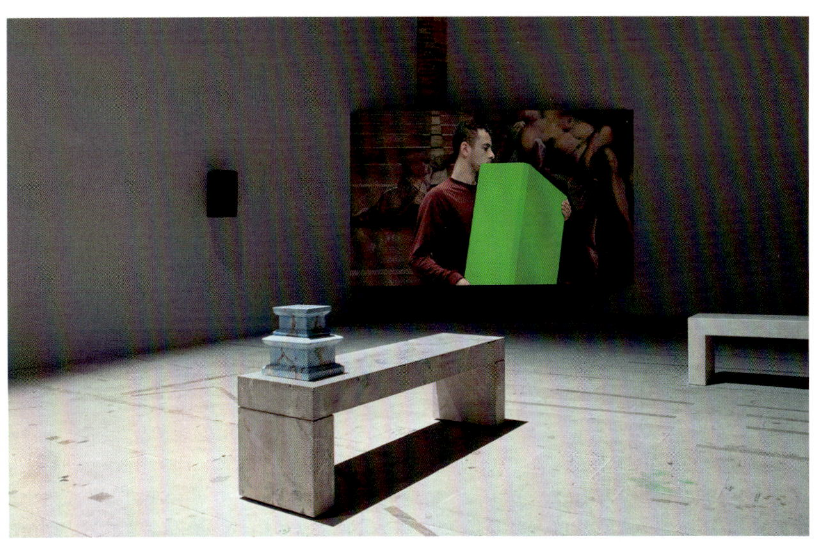

Not the Stuff of Stone and *Factor Green*, 54th Venice Biennale, 2011

agency. *Factor Green* premiered at the Venice Biennale that summer inside the massive Arsenale exhibition space, presented as a screen projection within a room installation of faux-marble sculptures resembling benches, also by Nashat. Though initially conceived as a mere prop, La Shape stole the show, delivering an alien shock to its environment. Catalyst, bombshell, disturbance: it was, after all, the green X factor around which all action turned. The thing nailed the role of nonhuman, nonorganic other. Its incongruity within the mise-en-scène proved irresistible.

Easy to spot in nearly any setting—in a crowd, a hall of paintings, against a speckled terrazzo floor or a human body—it immediately became popular in rarefied circles for its signature green, a vivid hue rhapsodized about by critics as "toxic, conspiratorial, seductively alien, and a perversely artificial take on the freshness of chlorophyll," or "the perfect hue for the impending Singularity of our technological age; the glaring green of an electric EXIT sign." While La Shape frustrated expectation by its refusal to key out, it advanced a forever-anticipatory, open-ended way of circulating in our spectral world. Throughout its short life, La Shape tasked itself with the monumental challenge of communicating with humans across the subject/object, person/thing divide, at once passively fielding and actively eliciting our dream projections. A born performer, it was equally at home in the museum and on stage, eager for attention from any audience.

At first, La Shape was simpler— childlike, some say. It began as a rectangular solid with four beveled edges, designed as a bastardized ersatz for a quintessential Minimalist, Finish Fetish sculpture. In this form of a boxy trunk, La Shape was more akin to the torso of a body than it was to the head or brain it eventually came to resemble. In fact, Nashat designed the shape in response to the central figure in Tintoretto's *St. Mark's Body Brought to Venice* (1562–66, also referred to as *The Abduction of the*

Body of St. Mark from Alexandria, The Stealing of the Dead Body of St. Mark, The Transport of the Body of St. Mark, and other similarly evocative variations). La Shape is an abstraction of the foreshortened torso of the saint's limp, twisted corpse, seen naked in the painting as it is carried feet first by three robed men. The heaving, breathing, and lifting of heavy flesh always preceded intellection within La Shape's anatomical evolution. Head, arms, and legs may be missing from the crucial object-body, but they are everywhere in the painting-filled halls that were its original habitat in *Factor Green*: throughout the many large paintings on view and certainly on the body of the video's protagonist, who unwraps the prop, moves it, sits and stands on it, hugs it, and sets it free to, ultimately, levitate on its own power. La Shape's debut told an uplifting tale of thing-liberation: a star being born, a divine resurrection abstracted as floating body.

La Shape's second appearance occurred in Nashat's video *Replay the Ruse* (2012), a traumatic and frantic family portrait of the five Platonic solids, which have represented the most "primitive" volumes in Euclidean geometry since antiquity. In the video, we see founding paragons of rationality through the lens of candy-colored crisis, measured abstraction presented as hallucinatory emergency. Many have noted that these shapes are so basic and planar that they could easily be rendered digitally, but an encounter with a master collagist in Los Angeles introduced Nashat to the art of stop-motion animation and convinced him that the solids must be built and photographed in the flesh. Indeed, several versions of La Shape were made out of MDF in four different sizes to fit

the scales of various projects, and yet, all physical manifestations are considered to be manifestations of the same singular being. *Replay the Ruse* intercuts dynamic studio shots of the five solids staged against lushly colored backgrounds (extreme zooms of each, in and out, repeat on loop) with scenes of two actors: first, a man (played by Adam Linder) running up a flight of stairs, who trips and falls (his head cropped out of frame), followed by a woman (played by Sonia Pregrad) seen head-on in direct address to the man and the camera, through fluctuating depths of focus, who delivers a short monologue (partly based on the words of Lorraine Daston). Both wear green unitards, demonstrating an allegiance or equal, sympathetic relation with the nonhuman characters. In its enigmatic muteness, the object slyly reveals demonic as well as protective attributes in this role, suggesting itself as curse and idol of those under its influence.

The pair of La Shape and the fallen or traumatized body forms the basis of a related group of four photographic diptychs that were

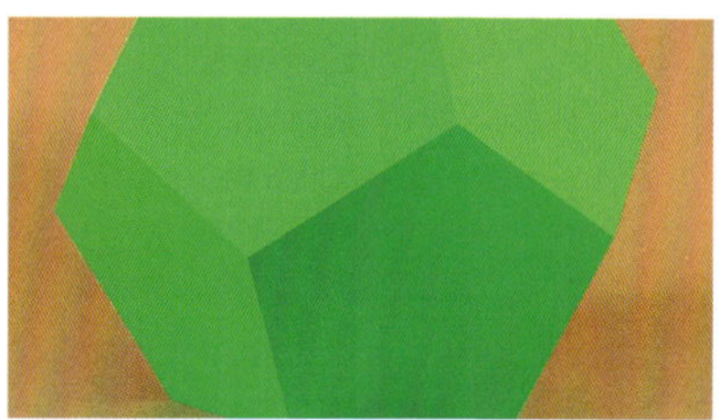

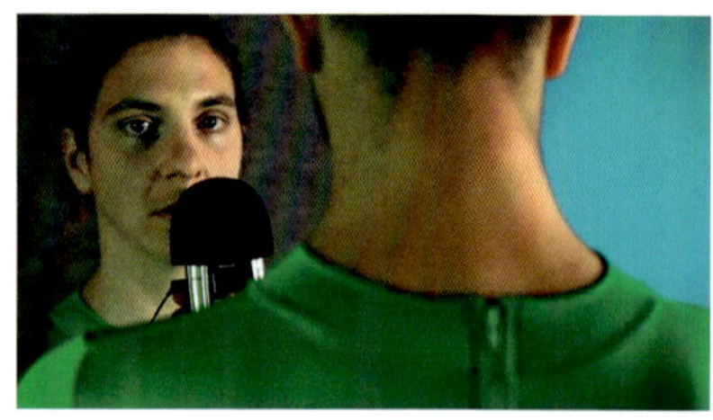

Stills of *Replay the Ruse*, 2012

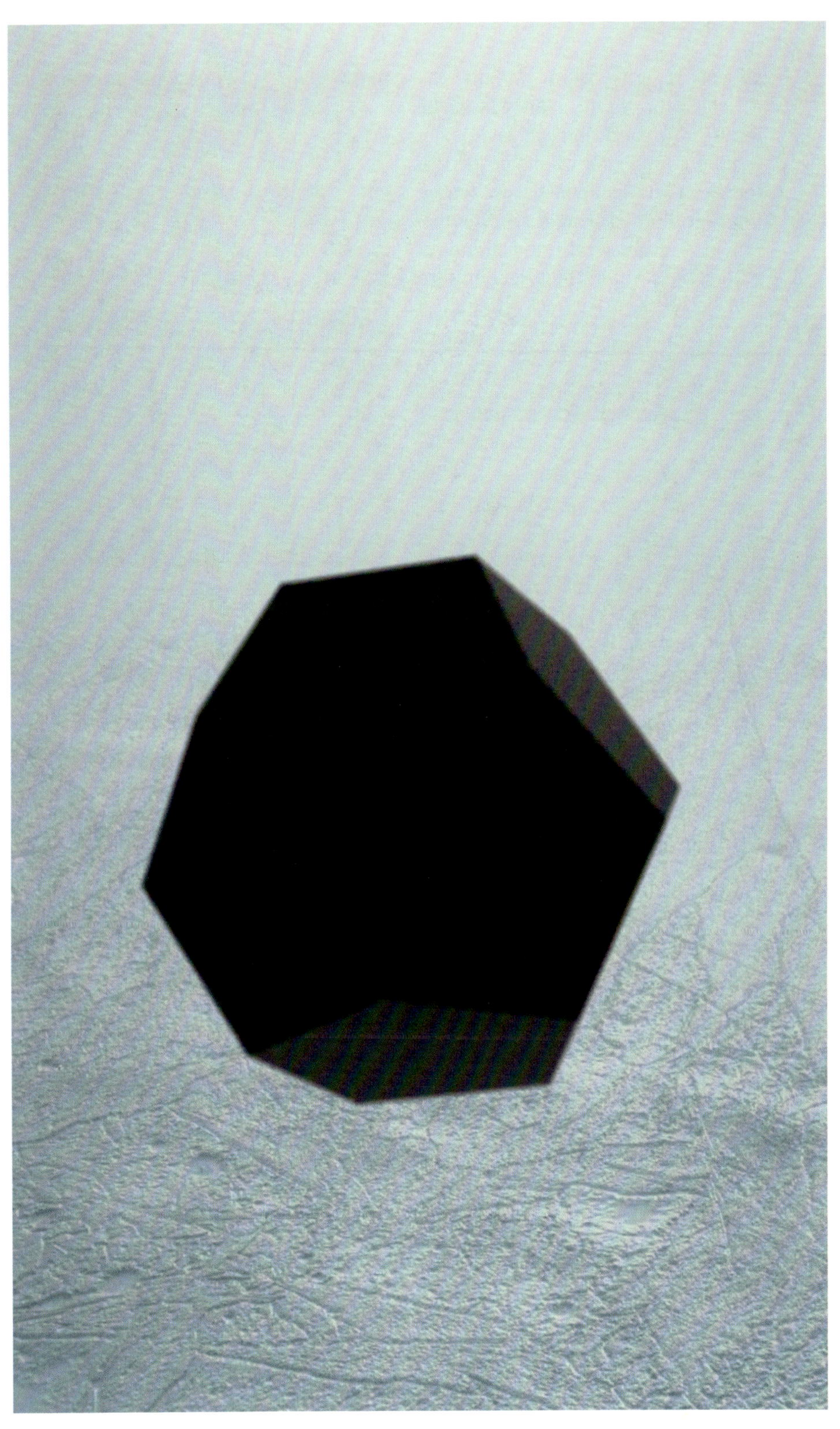

shown together with *Replay the Ruse* at Silberkuppe gallery in Berlin in 2012. In each diptych, a smaller, framed studio shot of one of the Platonic solids is juxtaposed with a larger photograph picturing a cropped detail of a body: a clothed shoulder with a small rip in the green unitard fabric; the nape of a neck where four

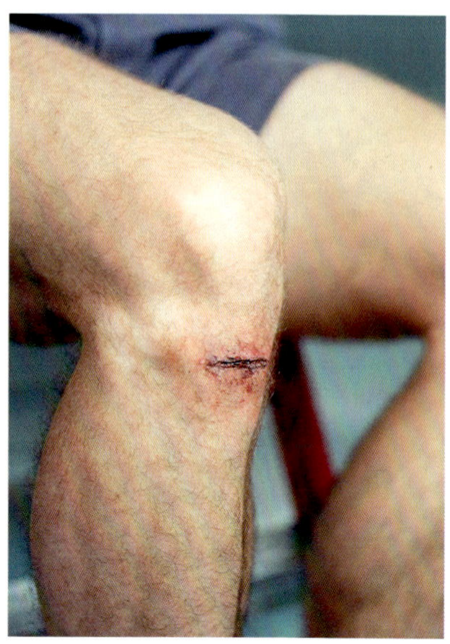
Change of Events, 2012 (detail)

hands mangle a zipper; a seated figure, also clad in the green bodysuit, with head and arms out of frame; a bare knee with a bloody gash. The thing never wanted to replace the human body; it wanted company. The two had to exist together, in relation and in relief. The incorporation of the body, often wounded, into these works came out of an accident in the studio. During the filming of *Replay the Ruse*, the male character tripped while running up the stairs, scraping his knee and crucially connecting the seemingly flawless geometric solids to the body's wounded-ness and puncture, actual or imagined or inevitable. The stairs, too—hard, obdurate rectangular blocks—assert their own crude thingness as an active force in that moment of tripping. The body's trauma is localized, sometimes corporeal and sometimes psychological. With poignant but understated titles like *Attend to the Wound, Condition Report, Lounging Before a Staircase Incident*, and *Change of Events*, the diptychs form an ellip-

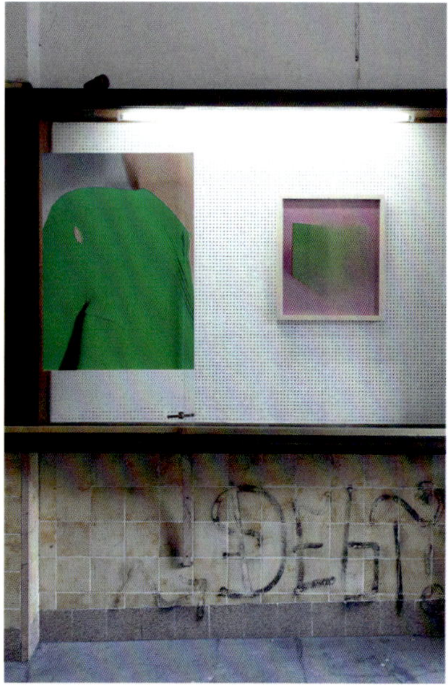
Condition Report at Silberkuppe, Berlin, 2012

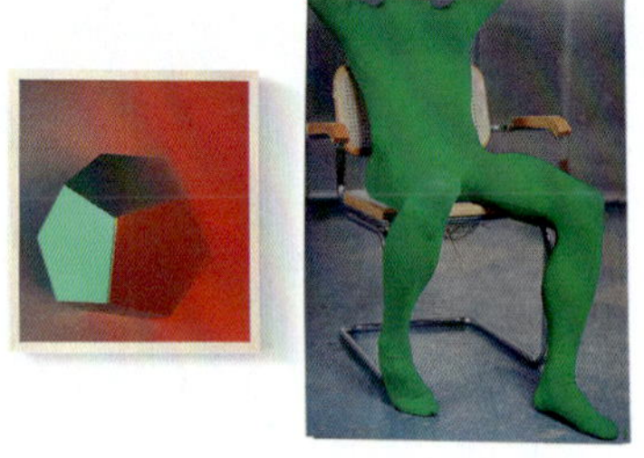
Lounging Before a Staircase Incident, 2012

tical relationship along lines of desire between details of fraught, scraped bodies and the adamantine perfection of the solids. There is the implication that the shapes' perfection has wrecked some minor havoc, that such allure always contains the possibility of rupture, danger, and force. In these photographs, La Shape is at its most radiant, lurid, and obscene, lit up and aglow like a rock star.

La Shape's career peaked with *Parade* (2014), parallel projects sharing the same name: one a live dance performance directed by Adam Linder and the other a video work by Nashat. Dancer and choreographer Linder recruited Nashat to design the set of a new stage work, his reinterpretation of Jean Cocteau's 1917 theatrical production performed by the Ballets Russes with music by Erik Satie and sets and Cubist costumes by Picasso. Nashat, Linder's partner and frequent collaborator, introduced La Shape as one of two "manager" characters in the performance—one American and one French—who functions mutely as supervisor, agent, and pimp for the work's three dancers. Linder, who also danced in the production, fondly recalls directing La Shape: "Incorrigible and hard-selling, chroma-green polygon brought a wry self-awareness to its interpretation of Cocteau's American Manager."

Nashat's video, based on Linder's piece at Hebbel am Ufer in Berlin, gave the prop an even larger audience. The refined drama this contemporary dance movie achieved through its masterful lighting, framing, editing, and sound effects added a serious sophistication to the thing's star status. La Shape's ostensibly mute presence was amplified in the video by an occasional disembodied voice-over—part internal monologue, part public address. Appearing in the video on a rotating platform activated its volume in newly dimensional ways.

Reflecting on La Shape's nature late in its abbreviated life, writer Kirsty Bell recently summed up its power and appeal: "It remains an inveterate proxy, one that generates only interstitial meanings, as either a

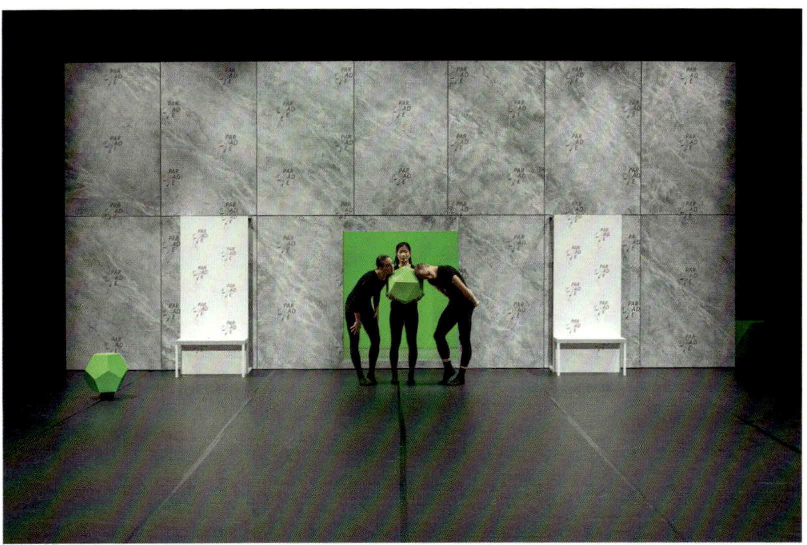

Stage design for Adam Linder's *Parade*, 2013

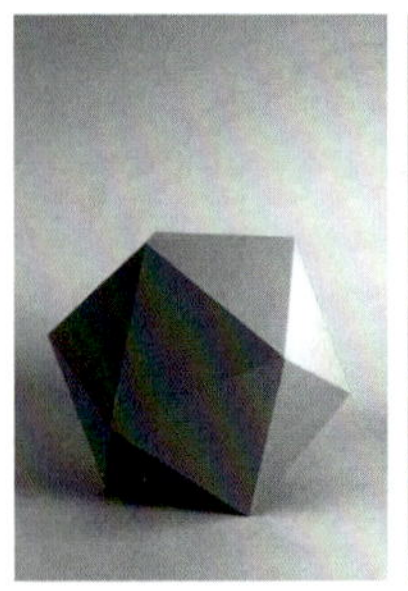

Evening program of *Parade*, 2013 (detail)

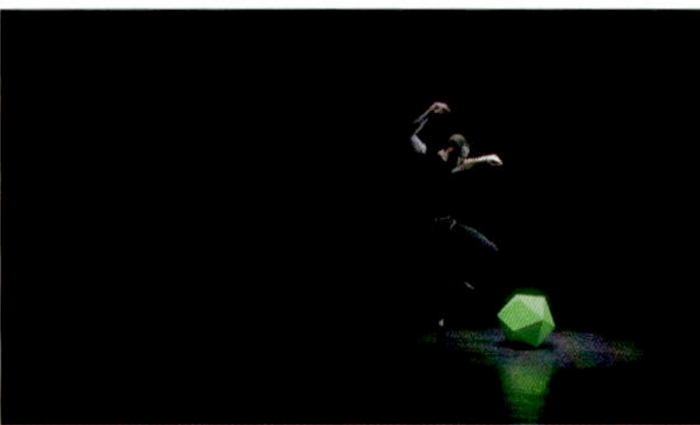

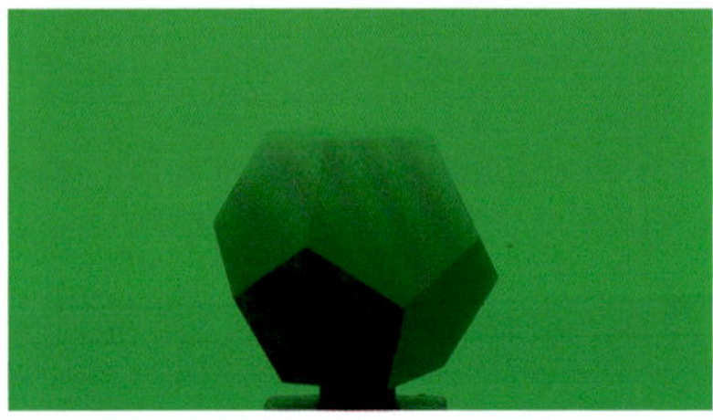

Stills of *Parade*, 2014

perpetual stumbling block in a partial narrative, or a prompter of the contingent. It is the sculpture as gesture, an object whose inanimate status is called into question by the variety of roles it readily takes on: an *artwork* proper, a token of exchange, a totemic object, a theatrical prop, or a character in itself—cast as the 'Manager' in Nashat's film *Parade*. [...] An object of fascination that refuses to give up its mystery, Nashat's dodecahedron is an incessant question mark in three dimensions."

Exhausted from the strenuous commitment *Parade* demanded, La Shape's well-being deteriorated. Its sharpness was worn down, and it was battered from weeks of rehearsal and damaging physical stunts. The pressure and anxiety of numerous live performances took a toll. The end seemed near. But first, La Shape's swan song: a scene-stealing cameo in Nashat's *Hustle in Hand* (2014), screened for the 8th Berlin Biennale. "It had participated in my work for about three years," Nashat explains, "so I felt it didn't need to play the leading role anymore, though somehow it did." In this final role, La Shape performs a relationship with the human so intimate, so lustful, and so vulnerable, that when one of the actors licks its face, it consummates, for the first time, its chroma-key potential to change color. La Shape's unprecedented and climactic transformation from green to mustard yellow was, legendarily, improvised on its last day on set, May 29, 2014. But, the change of color also corresponds to the change of heart Nashat reported feeling for the prop around that time, like a reverse blush. Feuds

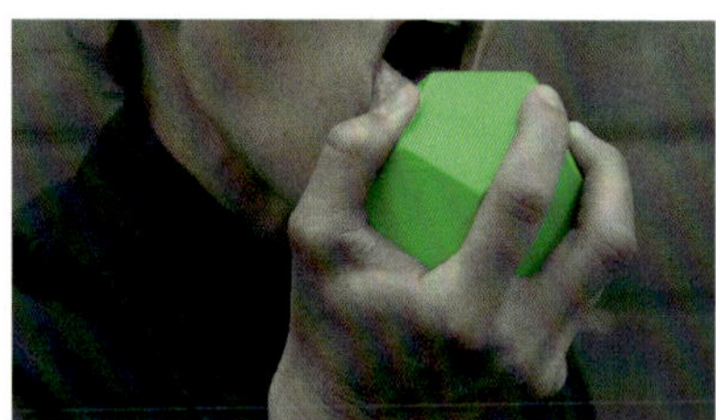

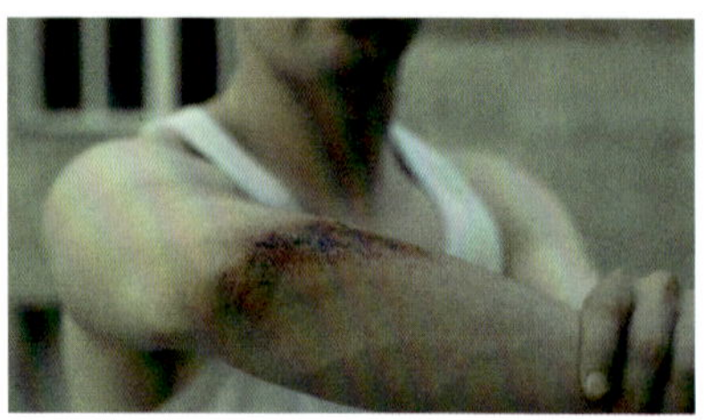

Stills of *Hustle in Hand*, 2014

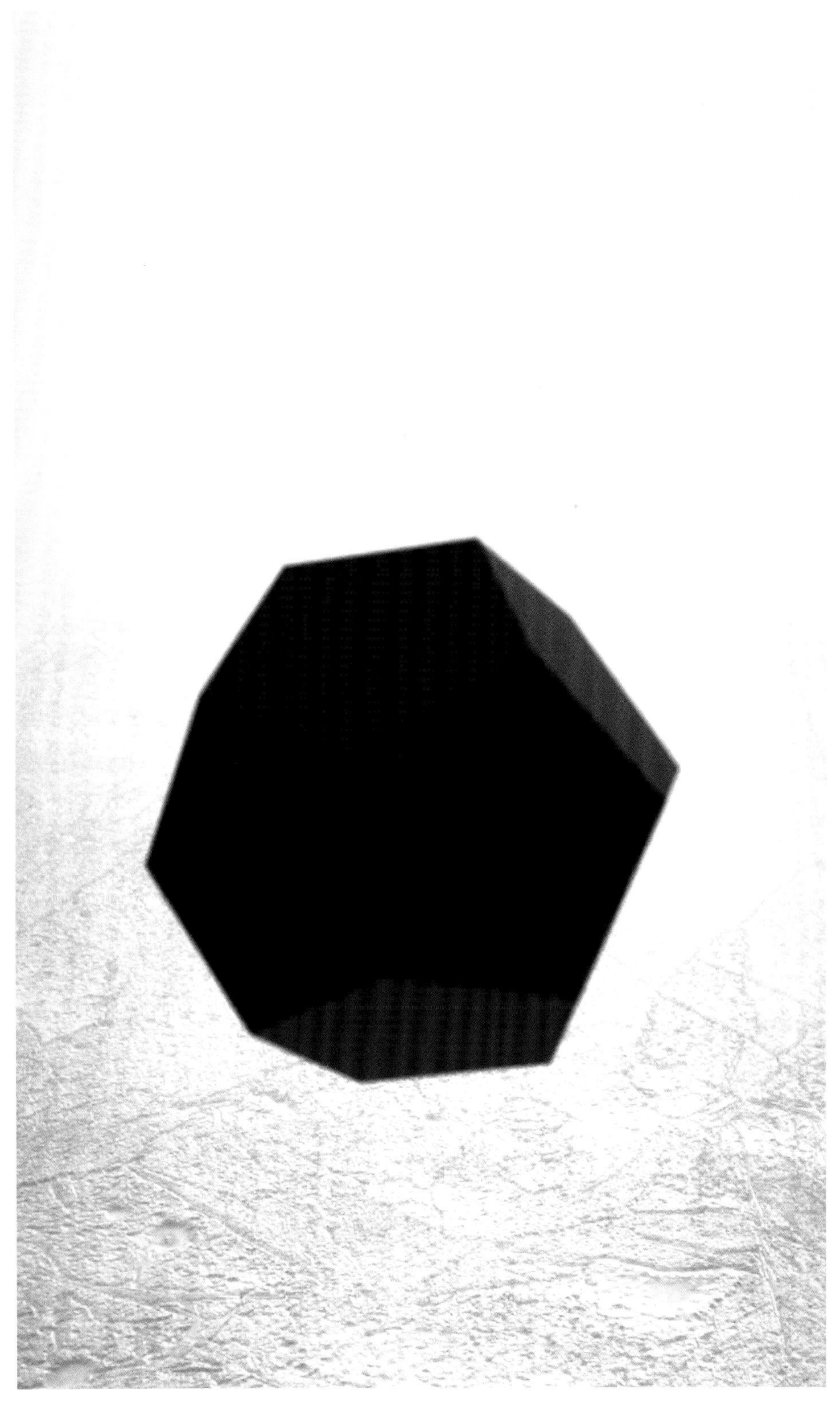

and tensions plaguing the protracted writing of La Shape's ghostwritten memoir (still unpublished) irrevocably soured the director-actor/producer-thing/employer-employee relationship. The collaboration was poisoned, their work together over. The thing expired three months later.

La Shape's legacy has already been influenced by the intrigue surrounding its disappearance as much as by its achievements in life. Rumors of sightings continue, prompting speculation that it may have staged its own death. But two dominant theories prevail: Some claim it perished from an infectious disease, a virus that wiped out the whole family of Platonic solids before it ultimately laid La Shape low—a new, unstudied illness thought to result from the emergence of consciousness in inanimate beings. The housekeeper who found its remains believes it chose to self-euthanize in the face of its terminal diagnosis and worsening condition. Authorities found a history of websites and searches for assisted suicide in the thing's Internet cache. La Shape was known, like so many sensitive creatures, to suffer from depression.

The competing narrative claims it was assassinated because it was consuming too much of the artist's attention, so much so that it posed a threat to Nashat's health, social functionality, and professional performance. La Shape exerted an addictive pull on its maker so strong that it twisted his characteristic good nature. In the opinion of close friends, Nashat's demeanor was altered to the extent that an intervention of some kind seemed inevitable. In this theory, La Shape's murder exorcised an overbearing, fetishistic relationship. Or, less dramatically, the murder was the result of plain old boredom as the artist naturally lost interest in the prop over time. No hard evidence supplies proof of either suicide or murder. In fact, the competing theories may not be mutually exclusive at all; perhaps they describe parallel and mutually reinforcing developments, twinned forces in play. The prop was found burned to death, a pile of ashes and melted chunks in the fireplace.

La Shape is not directly survived by anyone. Nashat, as creator and guardian, remains next of kin.

So the object had a life.

So it lived a little.

It existed, engaged in the world, and now is no more … Or is it?

I continue to see it, as I ever did, as a presence in videos and photographs. To us, it lives through representation, the embodiment of a fully mediated life.

La Shape was here and La Shape was there; it circulated and socialized. It appeared and materialized, always dramatically. It played these roles and it caused those effects; it had agency and sometimes attitude. It posed and it even spoke; it had desires and opinions. It was willful. It had a unique interior. It had a unique name. It came alive for the camera, hamming it up like a true child of the new millennium.

The question of being alive and being dead remains at its core. This thing is neither, but perhaps capable of both, moving between these states and flaunting the presumed finality of death … An intriguing proposition.

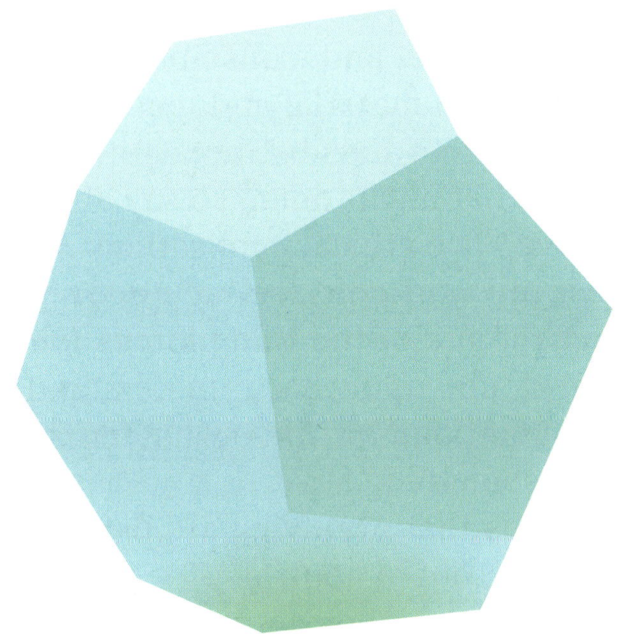

* * *

We marvel at La Shape's biography, and even more that it has a biography—or rather, that it convinces us of having one. Is there even much of a difference? There's power in effecting such confusion.

A consideration of La Shape includes the persistent problem of whether or not to ascribe life and consciousness onto things—both material and immaterial objects, concrete and abstract entities in the world. What might doing so say about being alive? The ethical implications of both sides, pro and con, feel acute. Thinking about the life of the thing forces foundational doubt upon basic understandings and definitions of life—what it is that makes something alive.

Things that are living are beyond our command, out of control.

Things are other: inert or mechanical, ambiguous or unnamed, strange and new. Is the life of humankind diminished or optimized by its own very thingness—which

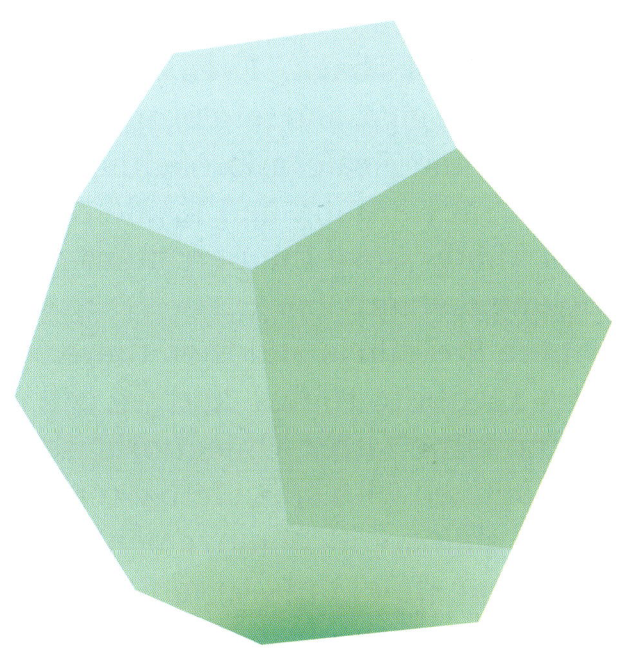

has everything to do with the fact that it will die? And I note, on one level, anything that isn't me is part or all thing. Opacity and inertia lie at the thing's heart. The farther away, the more thingy it seems. Objects are like words that way: they recede dubiously into themselves—as Walter Benjamin often cited, in the words of Karl Kraus, "The more closely you look at a word, the more distantly it looks back." Even as things balloon to mega, giga, and tera proportions, or shrink to a nanoscale, approaching asymptotic intimacy around and inside our own bodies, things have the persistent quality of looking distantly back.

There are things and then there is our mental access to things, and we will only ever know the latter. Object-oriented ontology, aligned with speculative realism as a recent philosophical movement to reckon with our time, opts to move past the twentieth-century obsession with human subjectivity and perception in order to refocus on things themselves rather than our access to them. For better or worse,

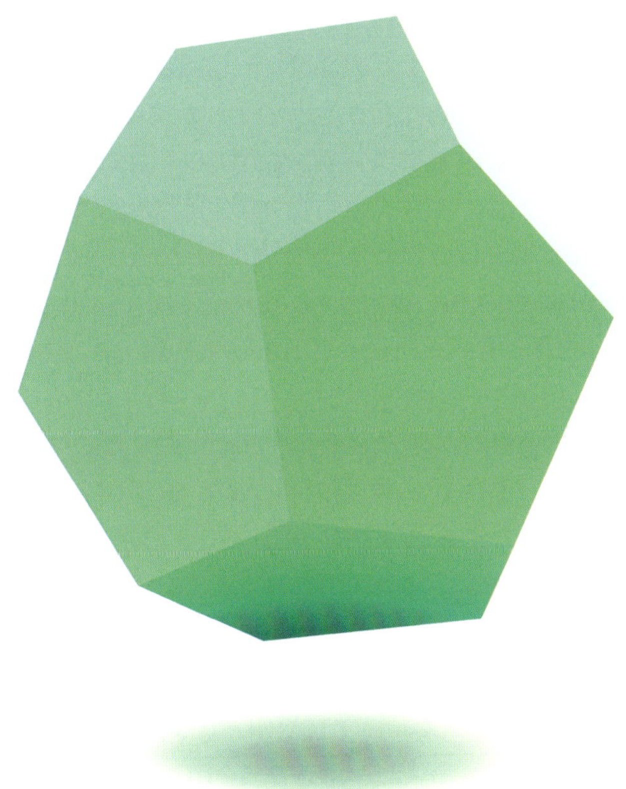

an emphasis grows now on *beings* in the world (the flat, utterly interchangeable "democracy of objects," to use philosopher Levi Bryant's term) over *being*, or our experience of Being. Indeed, when a hierarchical judgment of things is sidelined, it gradually becomes clear that access itself is also a type of thing, a mental object in the big universe of circulating things the way subjectivity, emotions, and physiological features can come to be seen as objects with origins and perceptible effects.

I too am thing-in-nature. The awareness of this fact comes to the fore of my consciousness on a daily basis. Especially when my arm falls asleep, ankle swells up, or knee joint clicks with every step—then parts of me are extra thinglike. When my biosystem fails and body breaks down, out of my control (as it inevitably will do), do I become more or less of a thing? At the same time, the more perfect and idealized a body, especially when photographed and posed at a distance like a model, the more it appears to be a cohesive solid figurine, the

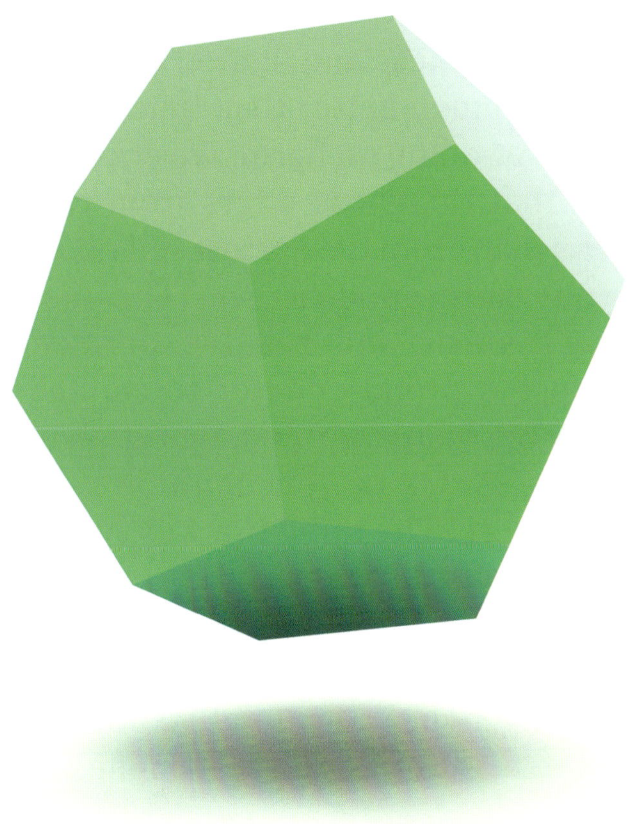

more aestheticized it is as a type and an object. Prosthesis begins to describe the ever-advancing hybridity of body and thing, organic and inorganic. Feeling seems to counter and reverse thingness.

But let's not denigrate thingness. No, shouldn't we aspire and seek to learn from its good qualities? Shouldn't we study its benign inertness and limited footprint? La Shape is much better than humans, for instance, at doing no harm. We crave the escape that thingness offers from rampant narcissism, from the narrow self-obsession of our anthropocentrism. The material thing's stasis and relative permanence propose a proud counter to capitalism's insatiable mania for constant growth and endless cycles of consumption … more, more, more! The thing is a way out. I want to leap in its direction.

I find myself admiring thingness in growing proportion to the amount I fear the hoarding, hyper-consumptive body politic of which we are a part. Thingness is, at

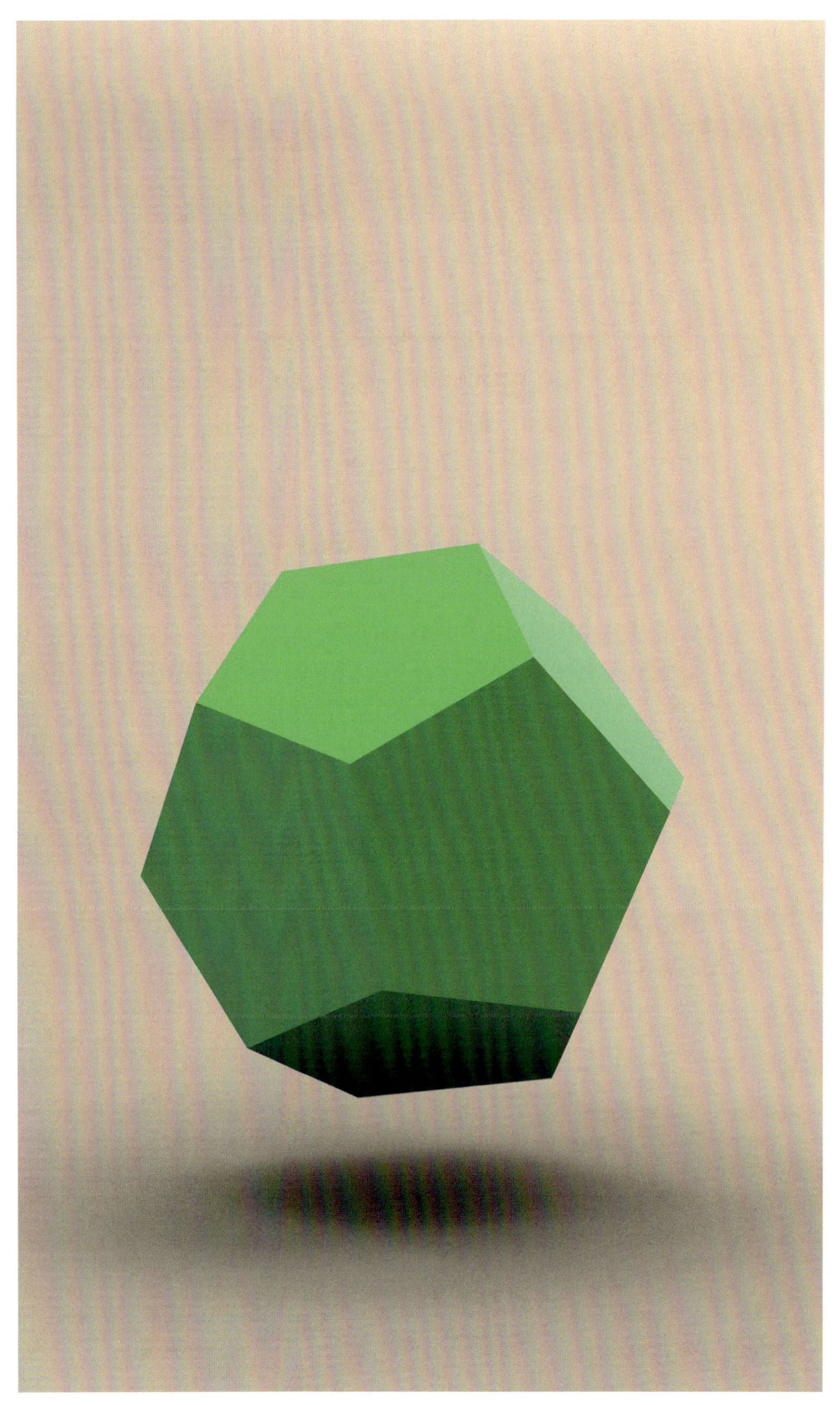

least in part, useful as a symbolic beacon of stillness, consistency, inertia, and non-neediness. In fact, for all its dynamic theatrics, supposed shape-shifting, and ripple effects, I am more attracted to the dullness of the object and more admiring of the ways it stayed the same over years and across multiple platforms. The attraction is perverse in a time thematized by fluidity, real-time metrics, and an overwhelming accumulation of data, people, waste, and representations. In an age of mounting precarity, so much of La Shape's power is rooted in the aura of slowness and formal stability it projects. It's like a big stop sign. La Shape models a reserved kind of sustainability; it has made its peace with self-imposed austerity and excels at generating desire from limited means.

Given the reality of the global devastation, environmental collapse, and mass die-offs underway, who wouldn't hate humanity on Earth? I hate us; I cannot even say how much. Humankind as a whole has turned out to be a vile, nasty cancer. We are

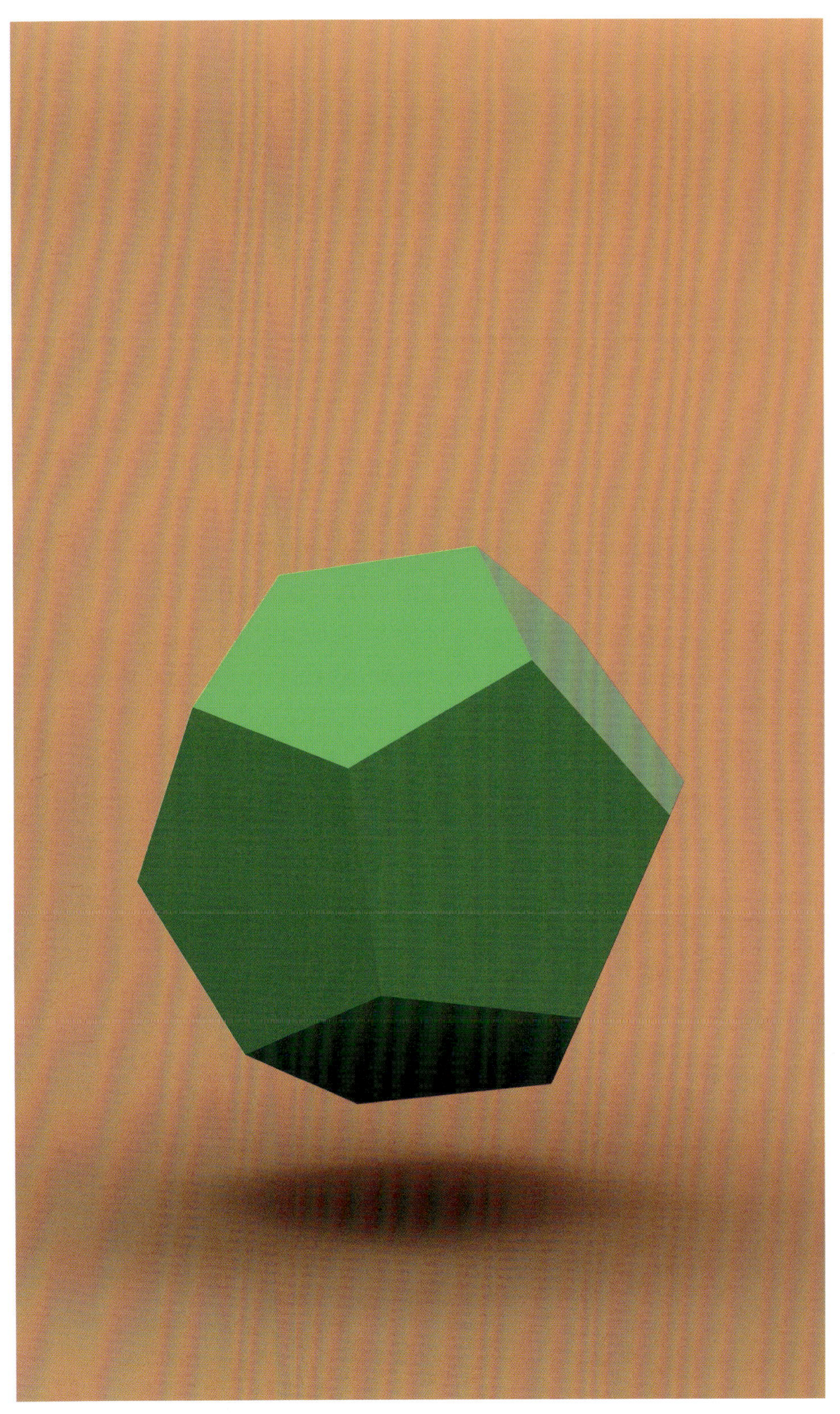

disgusting when we should be staging re-
volt and we are sick of being disgusted.
Sometimes I contemplate drilling a hole in
my head just to get out.

I keep thinking that we want, we need,
a way of interacting with the world that is
not based on the human and its parasitic
tyranny over all life-forms and things. Re-
sources run out; lessons must be learned.
There are limits that can't be ignored any
longer, we protest. Ways of living large at
the expense of all else must end. We are
desperate and look yearningly to the generous stagnancy of things, centering them
in our frame and placing them in the fore-
ground. What relief it would be to push
people into the background, out of focus,
or, fuck it, out of the picture entirely. With
things guiding the way, I harbor repressed
fantasies of wiping the slate clean in a massive reaping—you know, biblical-style. The
specter of death grows heavy in the air;
gradually, we get used to the idea together.
If I were just a thing, like a prop or a rock,
it wouldn't matter if I rolled or stayed put

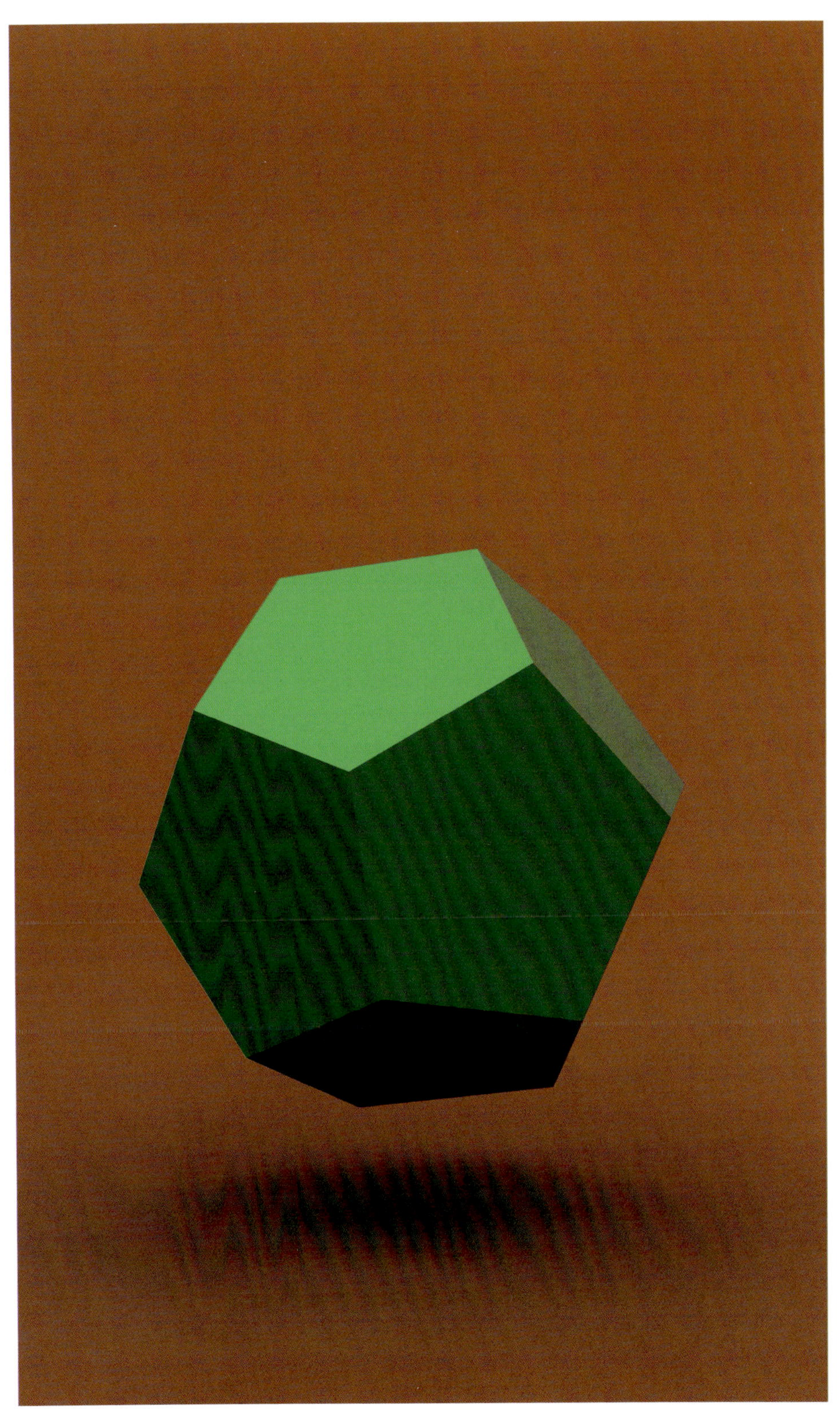

or sank in the rising tide and grew algae all over my body. If I would give up pleasure, I would also feel no pain. I wouldn't be in danger; I wouldn't die.

There will be new life after us, after we destroy the world. Things will inherit the earth.

It is not always easy, but we are making new efforts to embrace the mysteries of nonhuman material agency. Tristan Garcia, one of speculative realism's founding thinkers, opens his 2010 treatise, *Form and Object*, with the abrupt acknowledgment, "Our time is perhaps the time of an epidemic of things." It's our own doing and, furthermore, we are things—part of the epidemic. Garcia straightaway charts the razed lay of the land, the "cross-sectional plane" and "flat ontology" in which we live:

> We live in this world of things, where a cutting of acacia, a gene, a computer-generated image, a transplantable hand, a musical sample, a trademarked name, or a sexual service are comparable

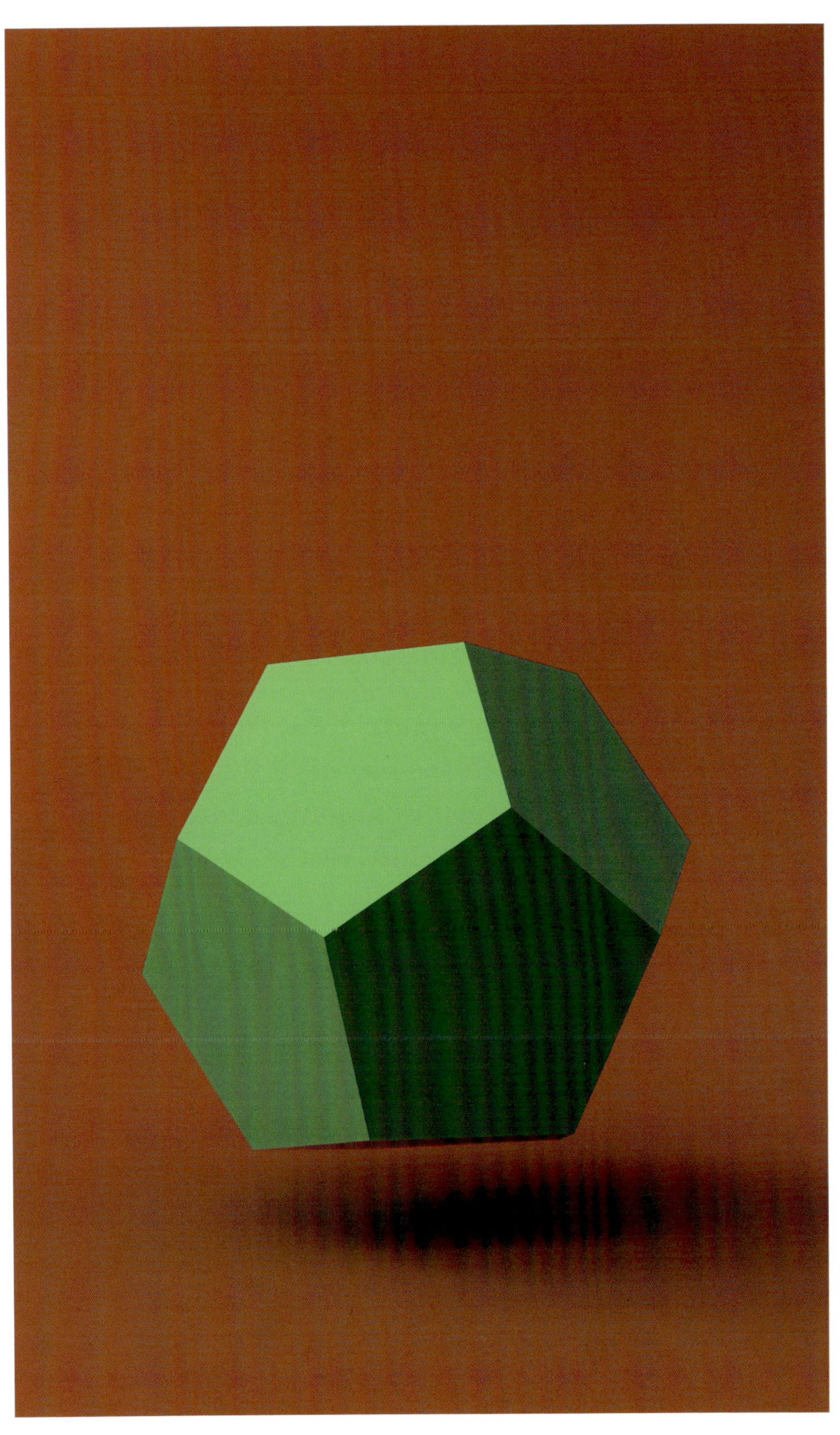

things. Some resist, considering themselves, thought, consciousness, sentient beings, personhood, or gods as exceptions to the flat system of interchangeable things. A waste of time and effort. For the more one excludes this or that from the world of things, the more and better one makes something of them, such that things have this terrifying structure: to subtract one of them is to add it in turn to the count.[1]

We continue to wonder how and in what forms we fit into the world of things. Similarly, La Shape contemplates, and makes us reconsider, how artworks are a class apart from other objects. Because, despite the resonance of such a flat ontology, there remains a difference between things—and that difference is a moving target, always in flux. Contemplating the cross-sectional plane should give some healthy perspective

---

1 Tristan Garcia, *Form and Object: A Treatise on Things*, trans. Mark Allan Ohm and Jon Cogburn (Edinburgh: Edinburgh University Press, 2014), 1.

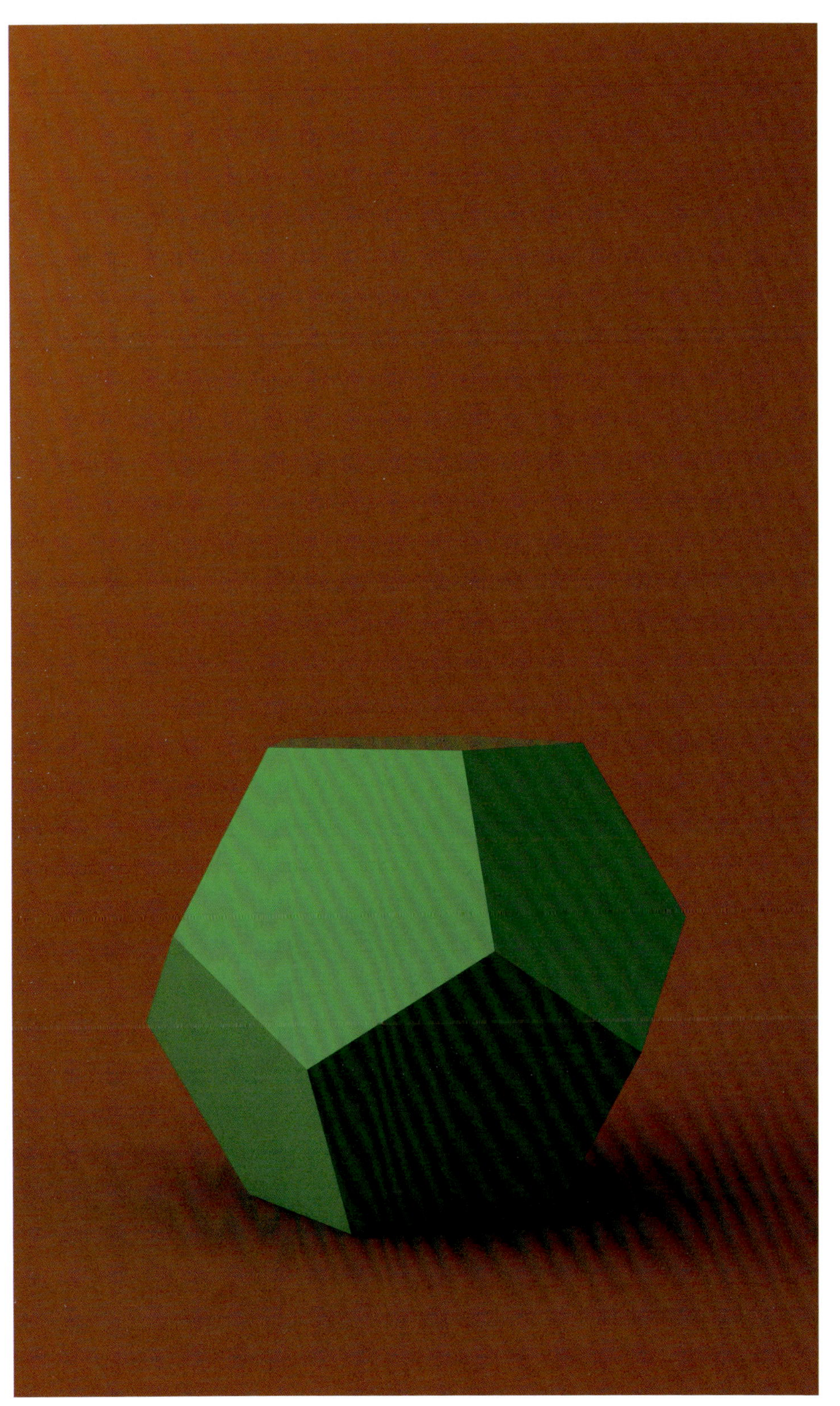

to humans and clarify my insignificance (a recognition not without its freedoms). It is this foundational assertion of, even insistence on, our individual insignificance that pulls me strongest to speculative realism. But the plane, which is a rather digital kind of space, need not reduce all beings into equivalent bytes of data, pixels, and robo-mathematical units. While we acknowledge ourselves as just another thing in the vast field of all thing-object-beings that exist equally together, we still experience the world of things according to hierarchies. It's just that those hierarchies of quality, aspect, and relation are constantly changing—never standing still for long. Another way to say some of this is that a philosophy oriented around the *thing* or *things*, rather than just human contact with things, would also be a philosophy formed by a deep ecological awareness and concerned with a vast and complex system of interdependencies that include but far exceed us.

* * *

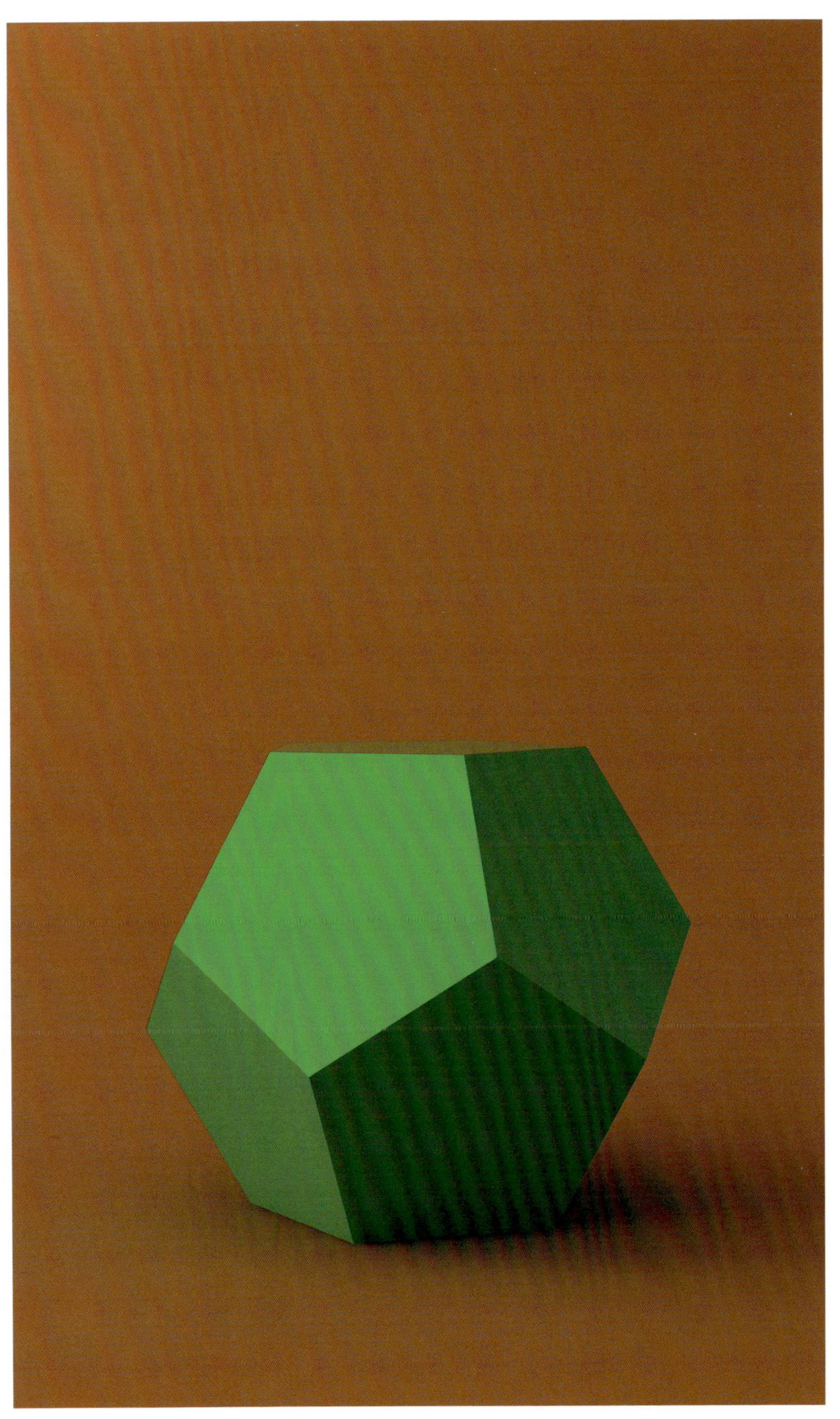

Tracking the object's biography also frames our physical reality in progressive terms of labor, exchange, and use relations. Stressing the organizing logic of material objects is a way to celebrate the common worker-producer while miming the conventions of luxury advertising, catering to a consumer class with fine taste and discretionary income. The object is always a battleground and history continues to be fueled by class struggle. Despite its best efforts to embody formal abstraction inherent to mathematics and rationality, La Shape cannot escape the real world context of class and capital. It depends on desire and aspiration. La Shape insinuates itself both through wide-eyed shock therapy and clandestine intrigue.

When, in 1929, Sergei Tretyakov called on literature to construct the biographies of objects, he was really insisting on breaking apart the perceived unity of man. The sharpness of the thing-come-alive slices man's skin and unleashes his internal fluidity. The psychological consistency of the hero is false and hugely revisionist. The

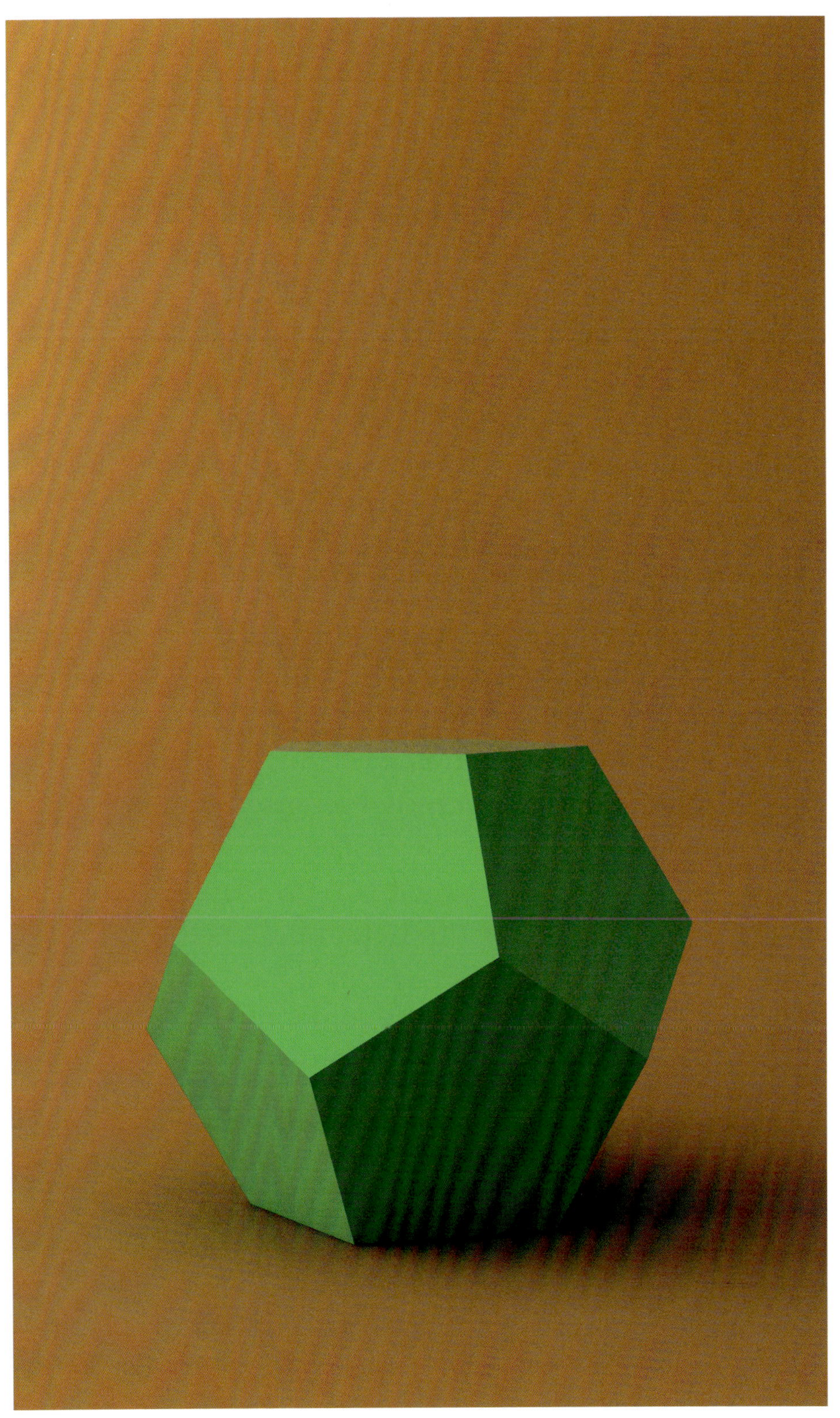

hero is actually a volatile collection resulting from the multitude and defined by all the production processes in which it participates. We know La Shape through the work and workers that made it and the work of which it is a part. Object biographies of the Marxist variety privilege the verb over the name, the act over motivation, labor over psychology. The living deed and its energetic effects are the main organizing principles, not persons or character. Individuals are secondary to the flow of things they set in motion. Plot developments are a chain link of cause and effect.

Such object-minded biography is more interested in tracking the movement of something, the way it travels through and learns from the many hands that touch it over the course of its life. Though the approach may seem cold and clinical at first, it by no means indicates a project of heartless accounting; objectivity is far from its aim. "In the 'biography of the object,'" Tretyakov wrote, "emotion finds its proper place and is not felt as a private experience.

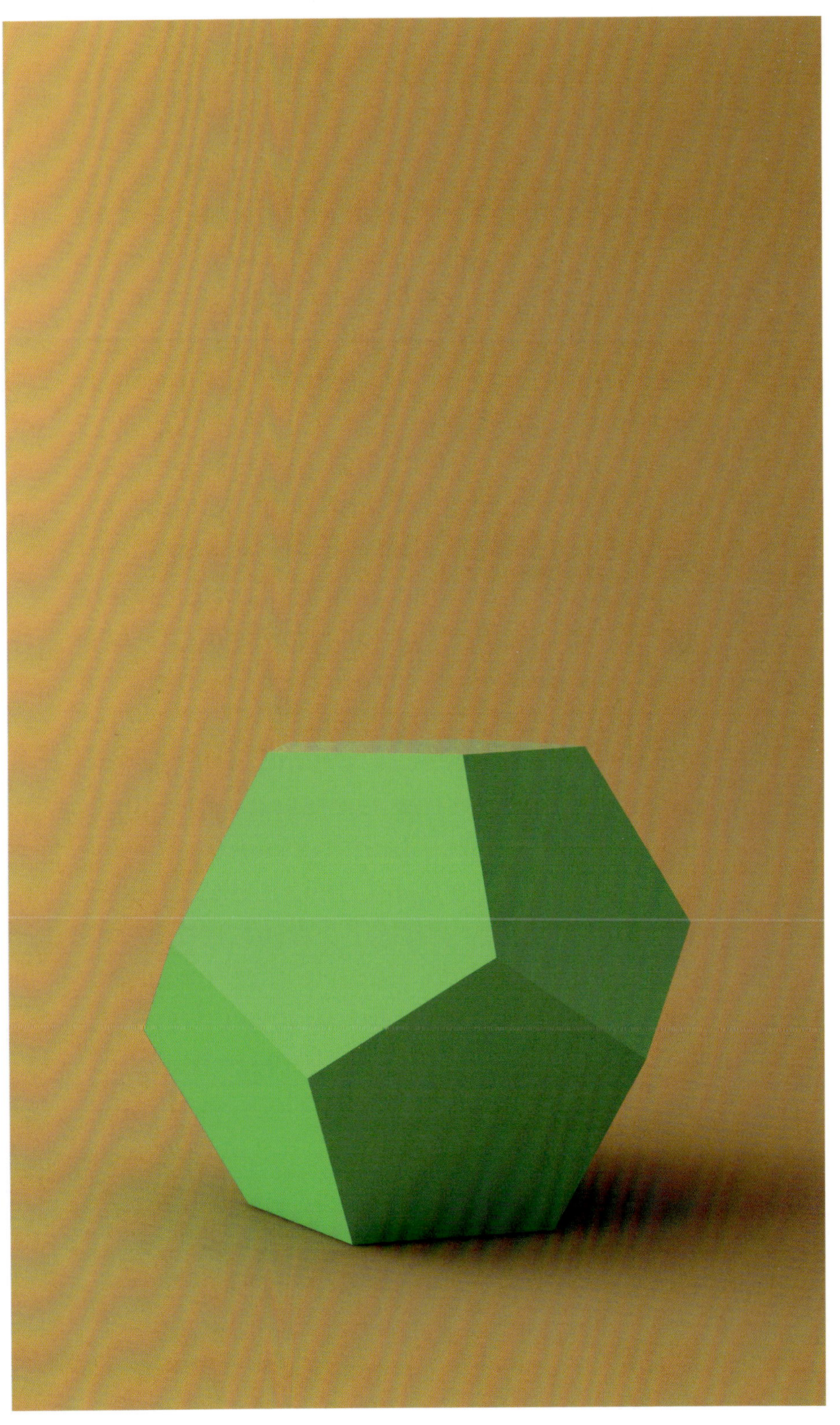

Here we learn the social significance of an emotion by considering its effect on the object being made."[2] And the effects are profound. I home in on those that are manifest visually and sonically in videos and pictures of La Shape.

When we see it, La Shape is sensitive and very receptive, absorbing energy and warmth from its environment. It changes size. One day it is as large as a big beach ball. Another it is down to the size of a cantaloupe. At its smallest, it fit in a coat pocket, or the palm of a hand. One of the hands it fit in had been greased with chicken fat and counted hundred-euro bills—a vulgar hand. The hand held it like a piece of fruit, an only partially rendered lo-res and pixelated object-icon of a green apple. The hand that gripped it moved swiftly and decisively, as did the tongue that suddenly shot out of a mouth to lick La Shape's

---

2   Sergei Tretyakov, "The Biography of the Object," *October*, no. 118 (Fall 2006): 61.

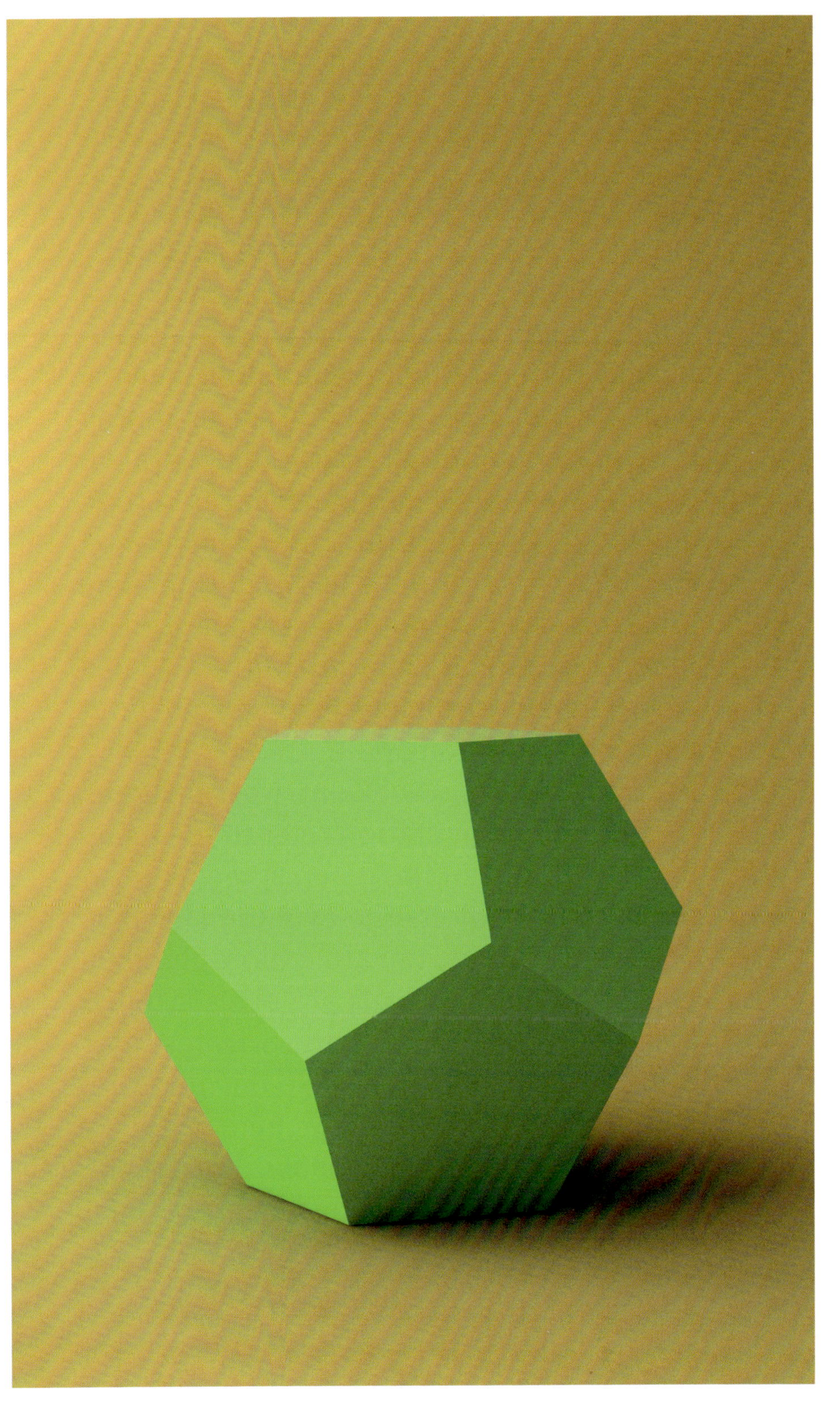

cheek, if we can call it a cheek. When licked, slow and hard, La Shape turned mustard.

La Shape is flamboyant; it strikes a pose. It loves to be awash in neon—reacting like a mood ring to heat in outrageous hues. Its hard, sculpted body seems to stay forever young and fit, but its appearance constantly shifts in minute changes of tone and light. The colors preferred by La Shape are highly saturated, with chroma-key green as the eye-popping standard. The look it goes for is "vibrant matter," to use Jane Bennett's term for things of such buzzing force and strong pull.

This look is no accident. Not only does La Shape's pigmentation refer to the imaging technology of the green screen, it also masterfully exploits the evolutionary bias of animal optics toward chlorophyllous matter: human eyeballs are extra attuned to green. It forms, in fact, the brightest part of what we can see because our photoreceptors are optimized for midrange frequencies—green and yellow. Two of the retina's three kinds of cone cells are most

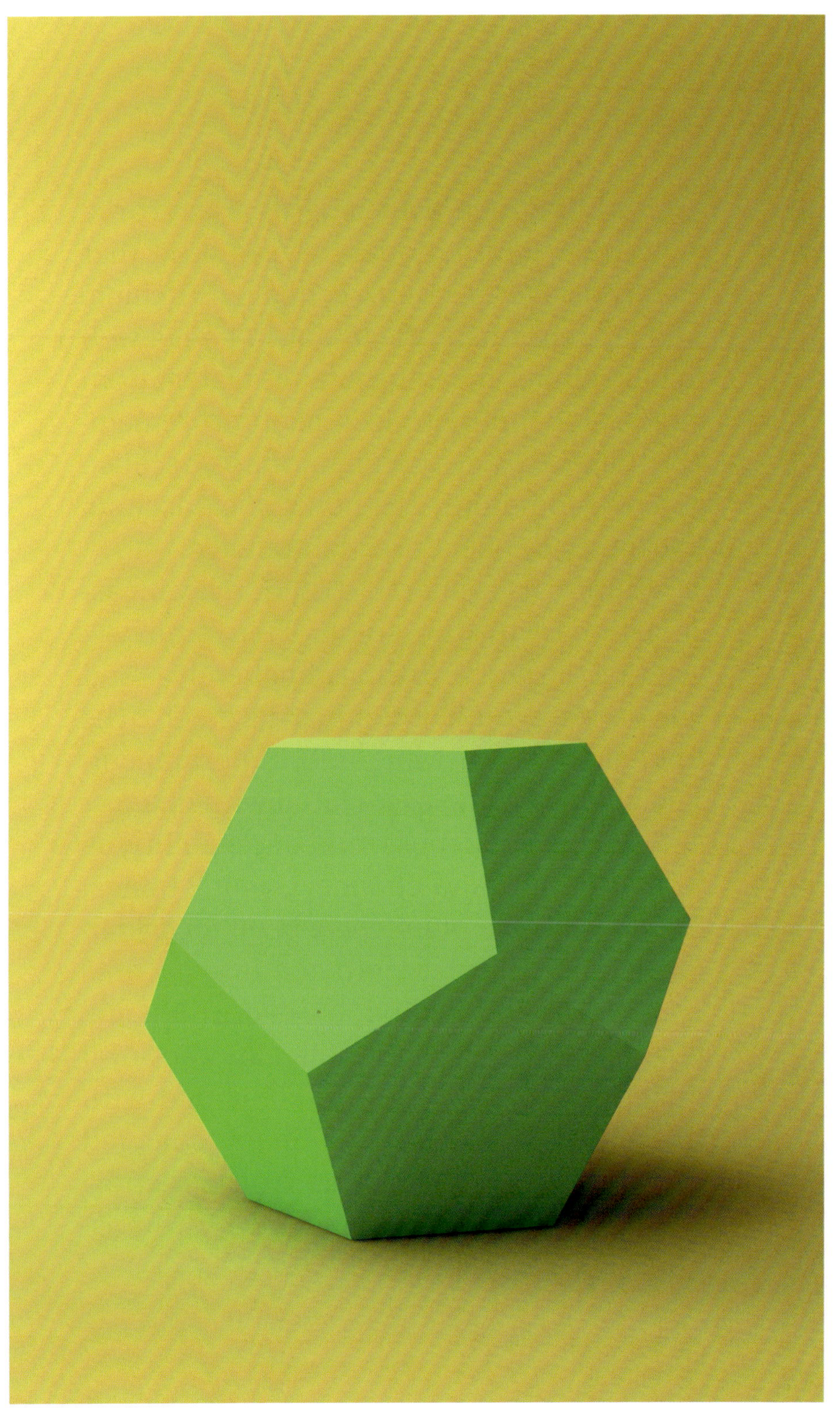

excited by green wavelengths. Unsurprisingly, then, international surveys show that green is a favorite color, second only to blue. And yet, curiously, green doesn't stick well to our retinas, meaning it fades fastest from memory. People are less likely to remember things that are green, perhaps because green is commonly the color of landscape, background, backdrop, camouflage.

Culture has generated other relevant associations with the color. There's envy—wanting too much, lusting impatiently—and unripeness, youth. Preindustrial green dyes tended to be unstable and impermanent. The color became associated with changeability, capriciousness, and unreliability, as well as money and chance. Gaming tables, from casinos to pubs, have been topped in green since the sixteenth century.

Color is also La Shape's endorphin meter. Emotion peaks chromatically. The aural dimension of its pleasure coincided with the one and only time La Shape changed color on screen. Blushing from green to mustard yellow, accompanied by the as-

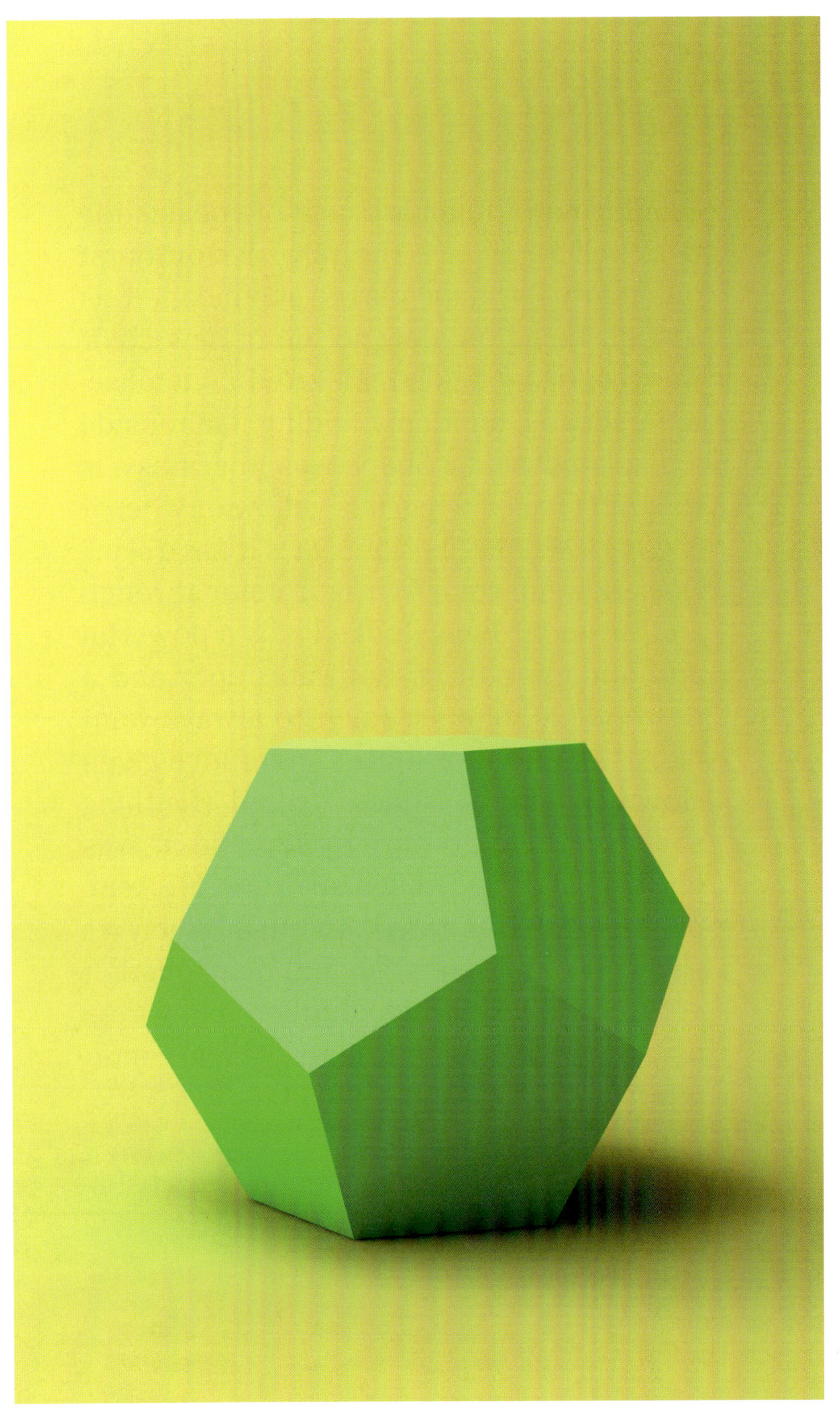

cending notes of a harp, a fit of vocal giddiness was triggered—the only such outburst on record. La Shape purred and moaned, as though being on view so full of new color was like being tickled. Elevated on a museum pedestal, suddenly finding itself inside a display case, La Shape was in ecstasy. Is the thing naked when it is yellow or when it is green? What is its skin? Does it have skin? Does it wear color? Or is it color through and through? Being looked at is a powerful and addictive drug, both an upper and a downer. La Shape seemed to always want more attention for longer, more love given slowly. When the camera drifted, the thing called us back to stay by its side. It was cheerful and saucy but also desperate, temperamental, frustrated, on edge. When we gave it what it expected and demanded, it got tingly all over and shuddered in waves of carefree sighs and titillated giggles, murmuring orgasmic oohs and ahhs:

Okay … okay … bzzzzzzzzz, zzzzzz, hahahaha, hahahaha … Hey! W-wait! Hm. Hey!

Hey! Hey, hey, hey. Grrrrr … C'mon. Hey! I fucking can't fucking believe this. What the fuck is going on? … *#%!^# … Ugh, this doesn't make sense! What the fuck is going on?! $^*%&*&*fuck%&*% C'mon. We're in a museum—hello! Hello! C'mon c'mon c'mon … I need this gig. C'mon. Yeah? Yeah, okay. You got it, you got it. Mmmm … Hahahahahahaha … ooh?! Ooh?? Hahahaha! … Well. Hahahaha! … Hahahaha! … Hahahaha! … Hmmm … Ahhhh … Mmmm … Hmmmm …[3]

The moment of ecstasy and relief is pivotal.

Sex redesigns the object's interior as it does our own.

Pleasure is decisive. Life is change and hormonal flux. Even as La Shape resists through all of its brute, inanimate inertia and stone-faced stasis, it does change. Inside and out. Lighting, for instance, is so transformative. Under the right light, there is no such thing as solidity; everything

---

3 *Hustle in Hand* (2014).

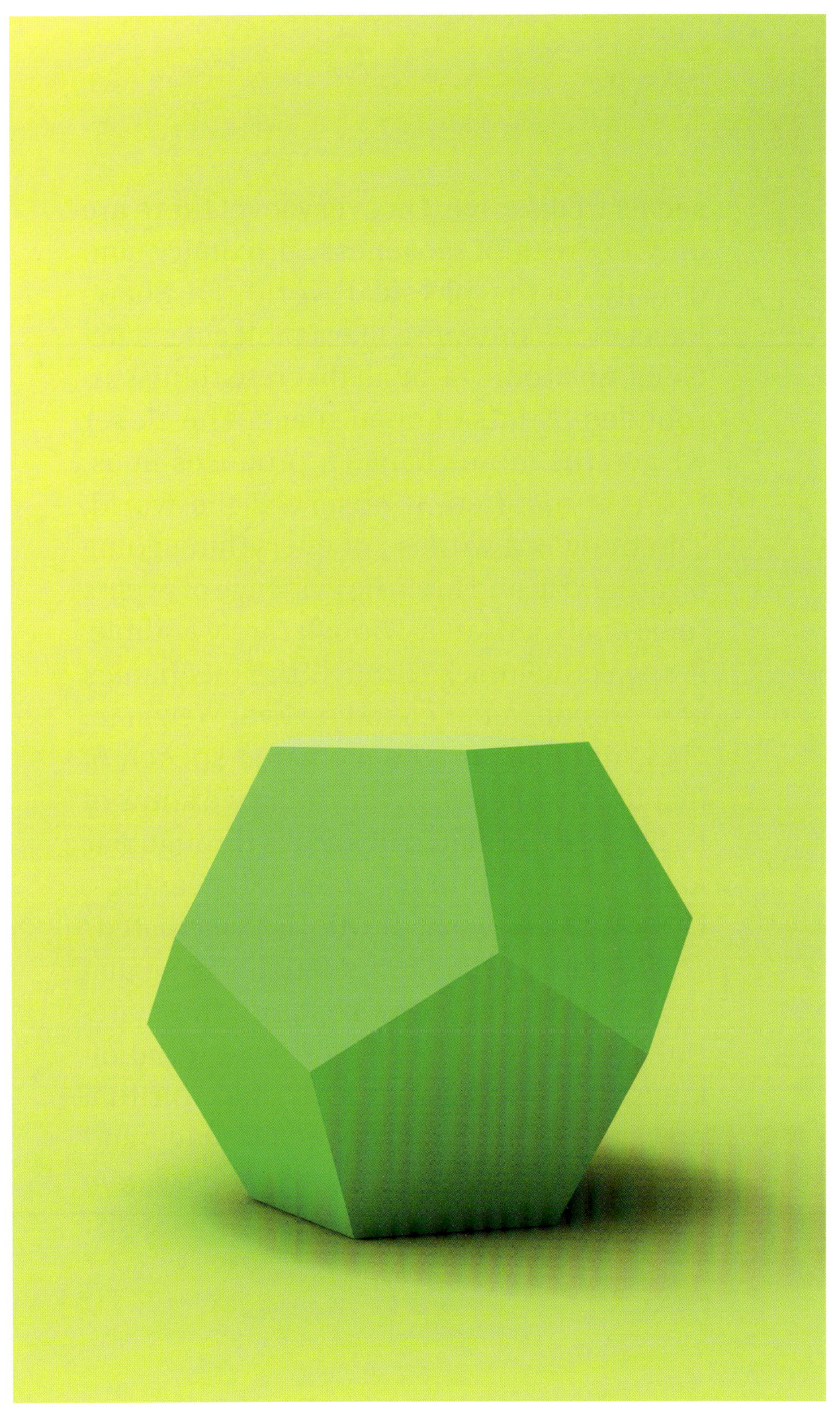

seems to dissolve. On every level there are only degrees of closeness, proximity, and density in the physical world. La Shape looks more and more like a molecule, a nucleus, an atom—a small discrete thing surrounded by lots of open space. The closer we get, the more change it produces in us.

As it matured, it observed the world. The thing is a witness of everything going on around it, and forensic evidence of events to be analyzed later. Though rarely audible, it speaks volumes through the mechanics of *prosopopoeia*, defined by Eyal Weizman, via Quintilian, as "the mediated speech of inanimate objects." Everything we know of La Shape is mediated. It speaks through our ability to read into its potential meanings. One could ask, what, or who, isn't mediated?

When it comes to its fetishism, sexual or otherwise, we can't separate the material aspect from the thing's immaterial dimension, conceptual gravity, and spiritual power. The fetish has irreducible magic and mystery, like a beating heart, *boom boom boom*, hammering away at our eyeballs.

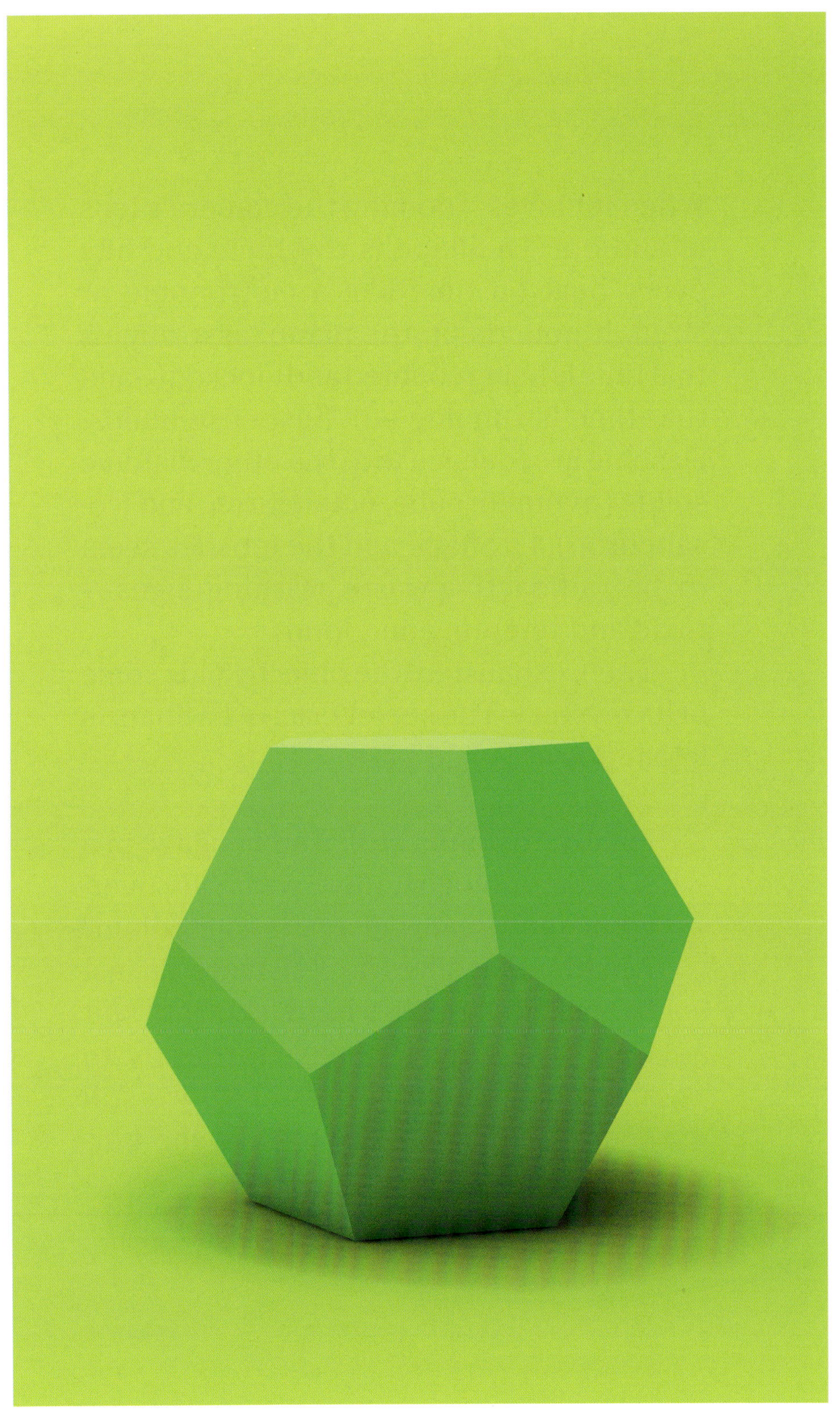

When it moves, zooming the camera's lens in and out, La Shape is rhythmic and hits every beat on time like a metronome or siren. It pounds on the piano, assuring us that time is being counted and clocked—and that time is running out. Suspense builds. Flashing in sequence with the other Platonic solids (pyramid, cube, octahedron, and icosahedron), La Shape and the fetishes seem to be radioactive-waste warning signs—toxic and tempting and loud.

Then, exhausted, the object yields some of its mystery. The secret crux of La Shape's fetish power is laid bare:

> Finally, it stands still. And I engage in a short monologue. Have we finally overcome our dreams of a perfect medium? A matter that offers no resistance against the will, that pushes hard facts into soft wax, that moves itself effortlessly to shapes dictated by desire. Do we still need such generosity to take the burden of our imagination?[4]

---

4 The monologue in *Replay the Ruse* (2012) is partly based on the words of Lorraine Daston.

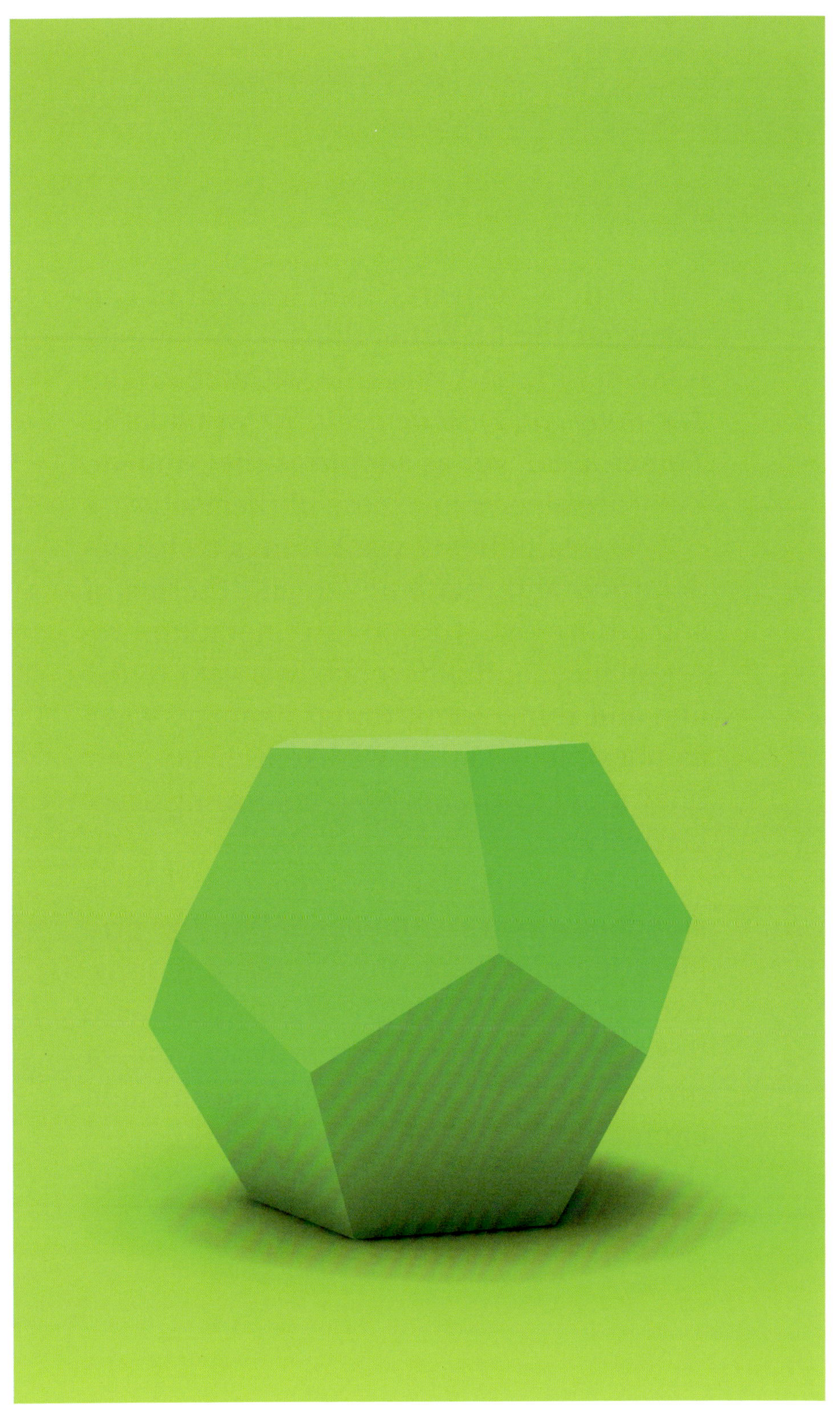

Still, little is answered, and we continue to ask what the fuck this thing is. Among its remains, I found this rule without origin: *The thing can't just be itself.* We won't let it. Things are never as simple as they appear. They are always in excess of themselves.

We instinctively want things to be understood and relatable—read in terms of something else, turned into metaphor, resemblance, and difference. We want to define and think about things as many ways as possible; whether we like it or not, our busy monkey brains keep chattering associatively.

So let's read La Shape's generous twelve-sidedness as a recommendation for proliferating angles and plural interpretations. We want to take on La Shape now as a descriptive project and provocation—a project that blooms in the mind through enumeration and growing lists. Here are three dozen ways to consider the particularity of this thing's thingness:

1)

LA SHAPE IS A SCULPTURE
WITH ART HISTORICAL LINEAGE
AND CONTEMPORARY PEERS.

2)

LA SHAPE IS PROP AND
PEDESTAL—IN A MUSEUM, GALLERY,
STUDIO, OR THEATER CONTEXT.

3)

LA SHAPE IS A BUILT THING,
A HARD BODY, A PREMEDITATED
FIGURE OF DESIGN AND LABOR.

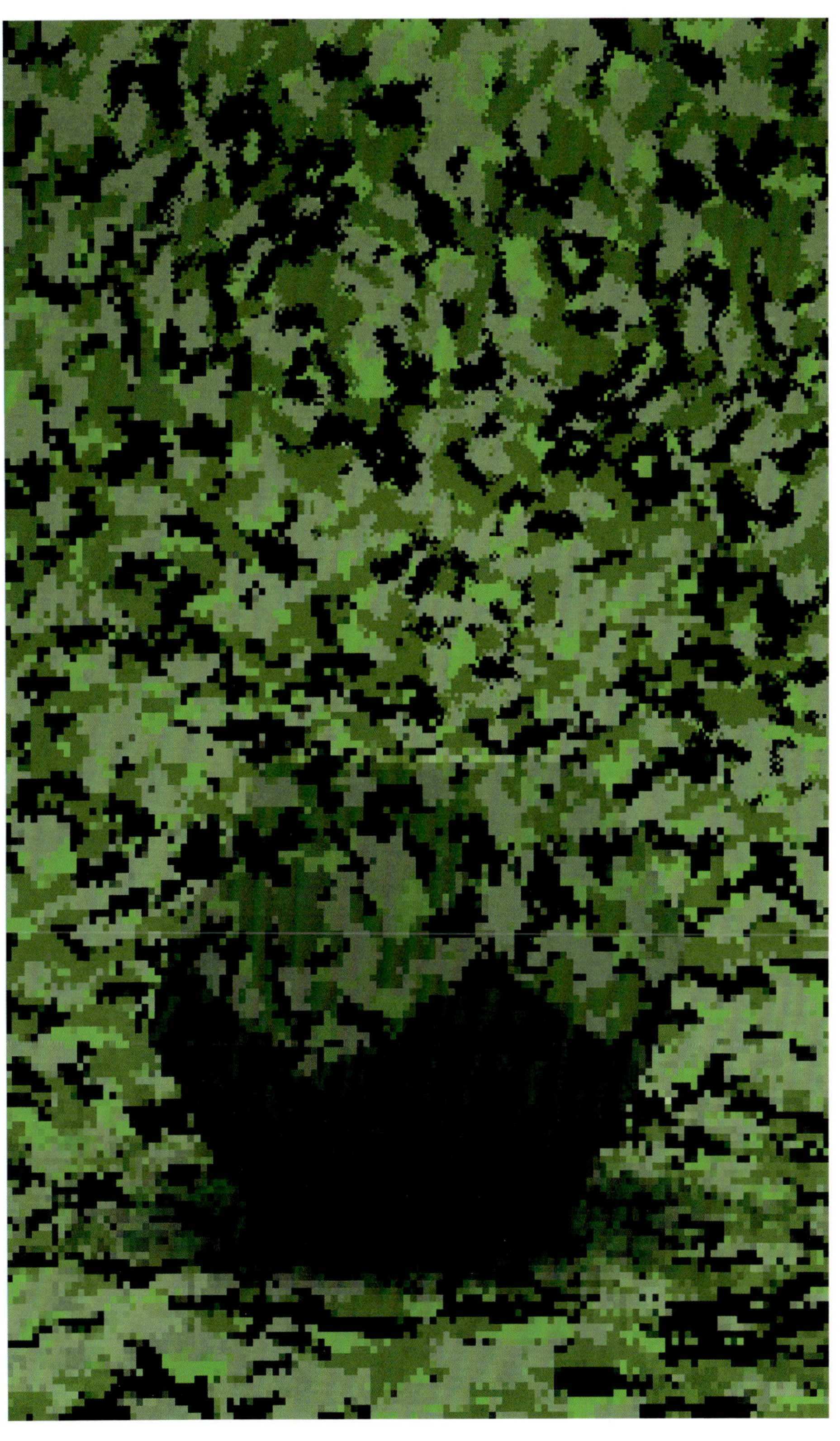

4)

LA SHAPE IS DEVICE, MACHINE, AND TOOL.[5]

5)

LA SHAPE IS ARTIFACT, EVIDENCE, AND REMAINS.

6)

LA SHAPE IS MASS, WEIGHT, VOLUME, AND PHYSICS.

---

5   It works to reveal us to ourselves or to convey, through its indifference, our insignificance. It is a technology and its opaque, magic shape is wholly in sync with the trend of technologies toward more aesthetic and more disguised secret cells. It makes me realize that it is getting harder and harder to even recognize an object as technological or digital by sight. It seems like anything could power up, beep, and blink without warning.

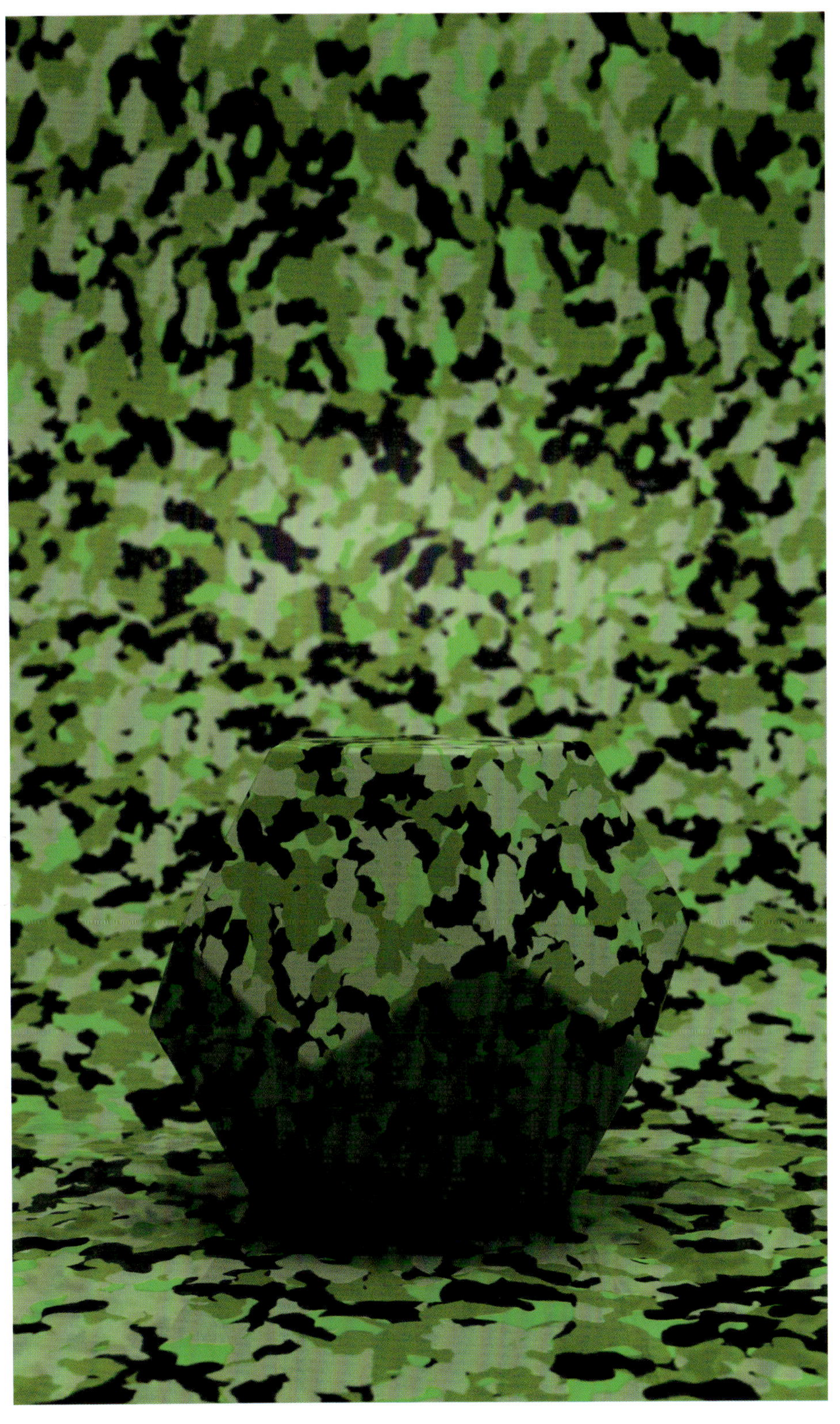

7)

LA SHAPE IS AN IDEALIZED IMAGINED FIGURE, A PLATONIC SOLID THAT IS WEIGHTLESS AND BUOYANT LIKE A SOAP BUBBLE IN THE MIND.[6]

8)

LA SHAPE IS GEOMETRY, SHAPE, AND SHAPE-SHIFTER.[7]

---

6   A dodecahedron is fitted with twelve equal, pentagonal sides, one for each month of the year and each sign in the zodiac. Classically speaking, it's a symbol of perfection and the universe's harmonious order. For Plato, it represented the perfect medium, able to encompass all things.

7   It stays the same more than it changes, but what persists is its green-screen promise of infinite new looks, untold equations, and solutions. It is math and topology.

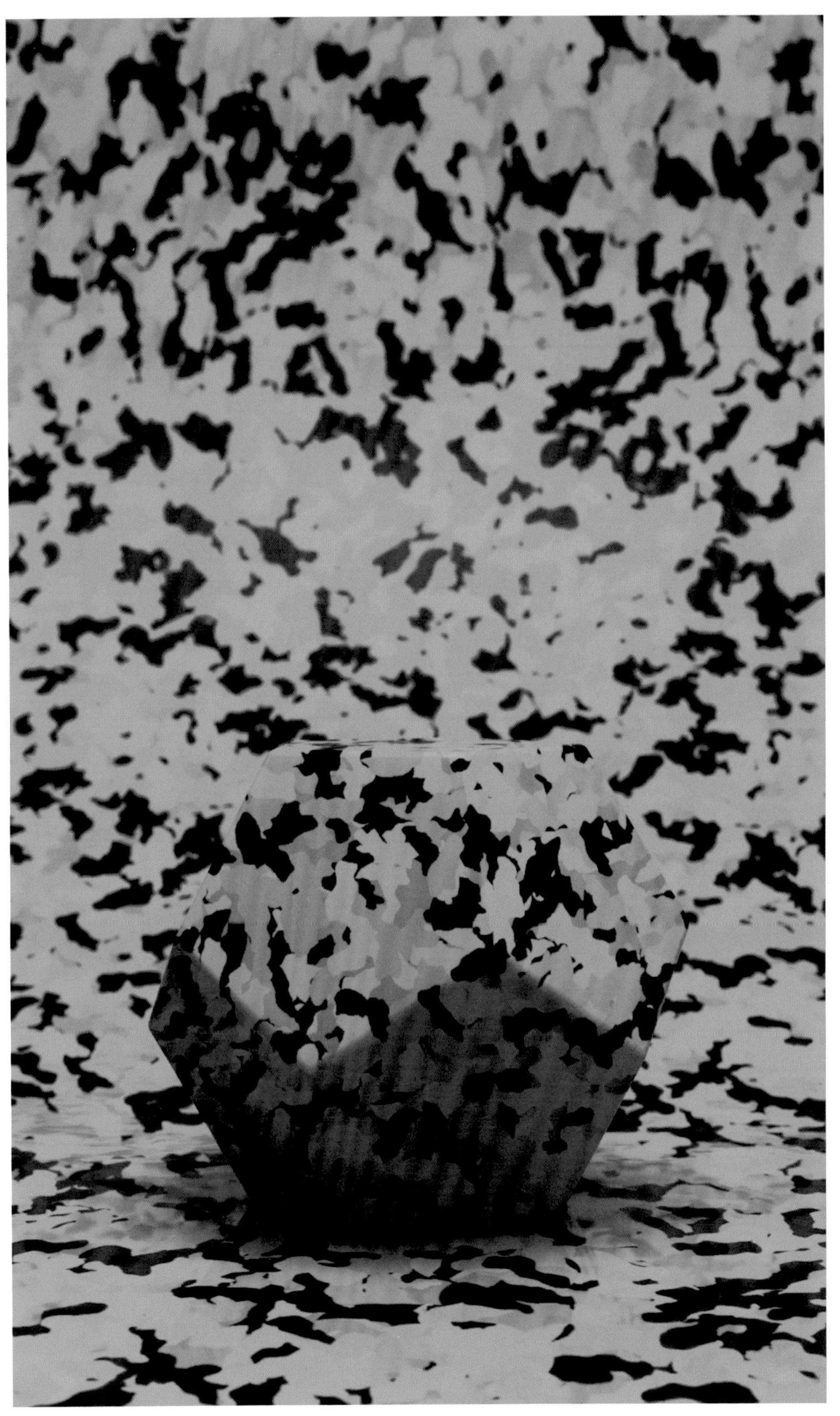

9)

**LA SHAPE IS AN ANATOMICAL
COMPONENT—A KNEECAP OR BALL
WITHOUT ITS SOCKET.**

10)

**LA SHAPE IS A SOCCER-ESQUE PLAYING BALL,
OBJECT OF THE GAME.**

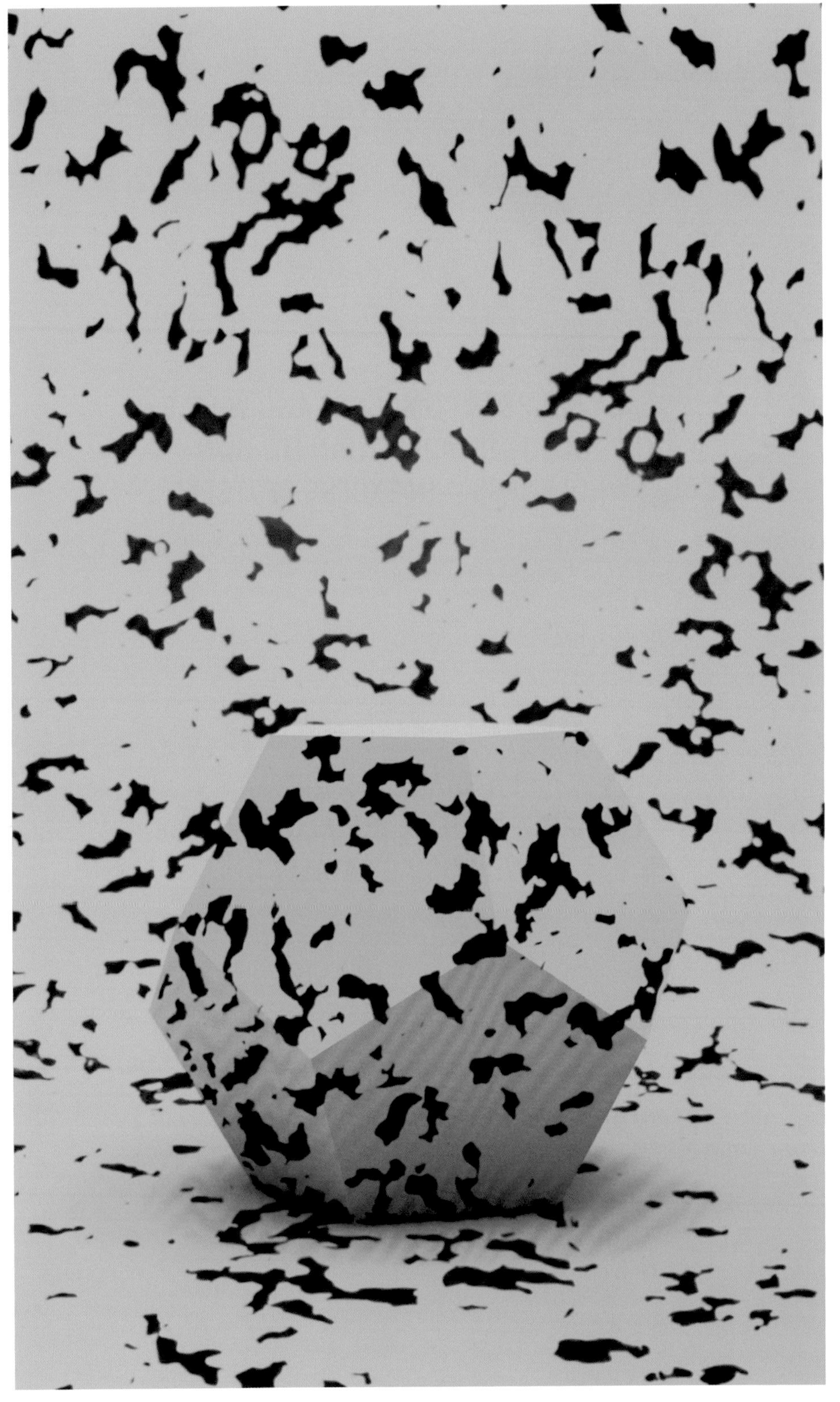

11)

LA SHAPE IS COMPLETE AND WHOLE BUT IT IS MORE THAN ITS OWN WHOLENESS—IN EXCESS OF ITSELF.[8]

12)

LA SHAPE IS A GIFT, EXCHANGE OBJECT, CURRENCY, TRADE, AND SOCIAL CATALYST.

---

8   Any thing is irreducible to what it contains and the context it is in. Garcia writes, "A thing is nothing other than the difference between *that which is in this thing and that in which this thing is*" (*Form and Object*, 13).

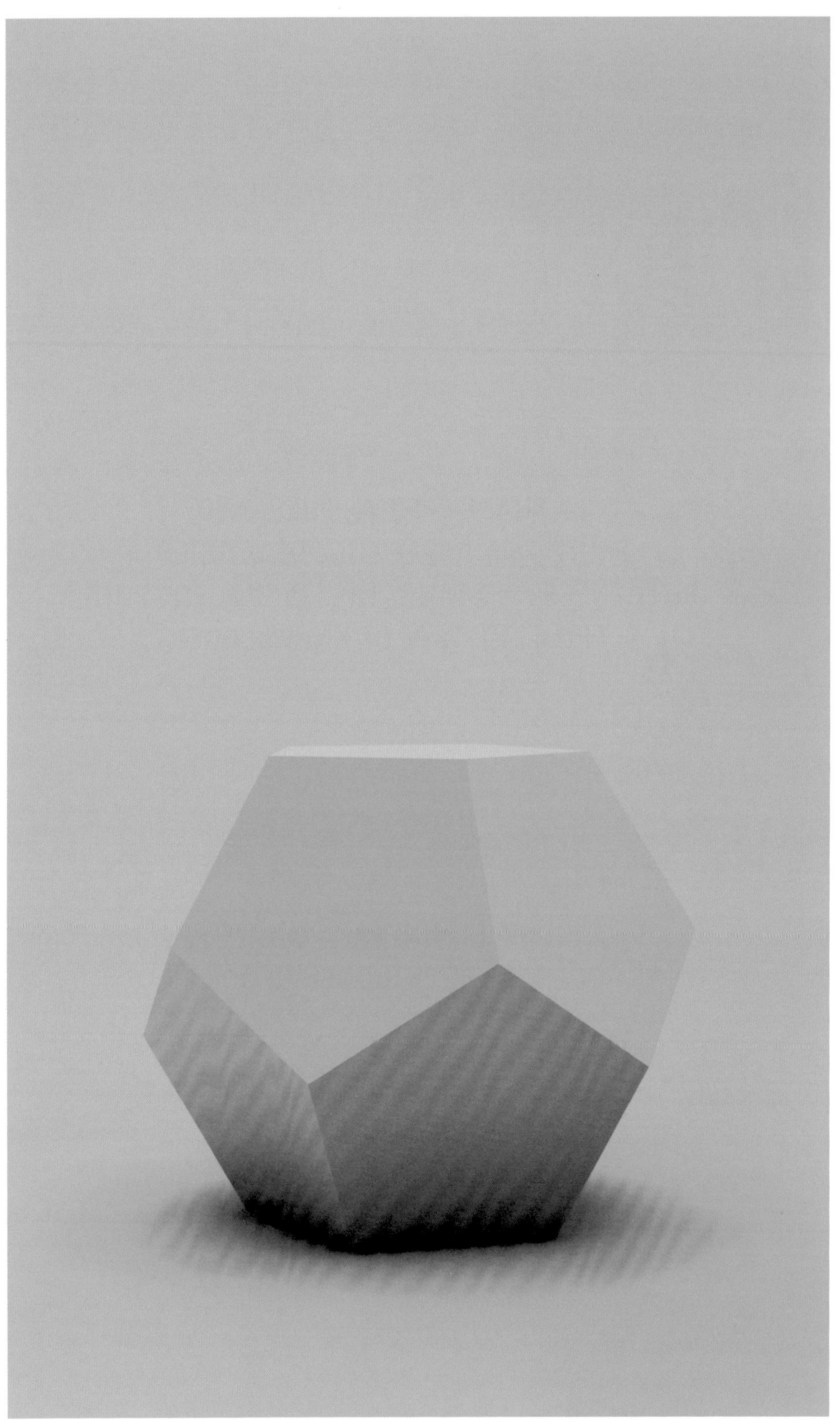

13)

LA SHAPE IS FOOD, FUEL, AND
FRUIT—AN APPLE FULL OF DESIRED
SWEETNESS AND TANG, THE FORBIDDEN FRUIT
FROM THE TREE OF KNOWLEDGE.

14)

LA SHAPE IS MINERAL—A FACETED
GEMSTONE, A HIDDEN GEODE.

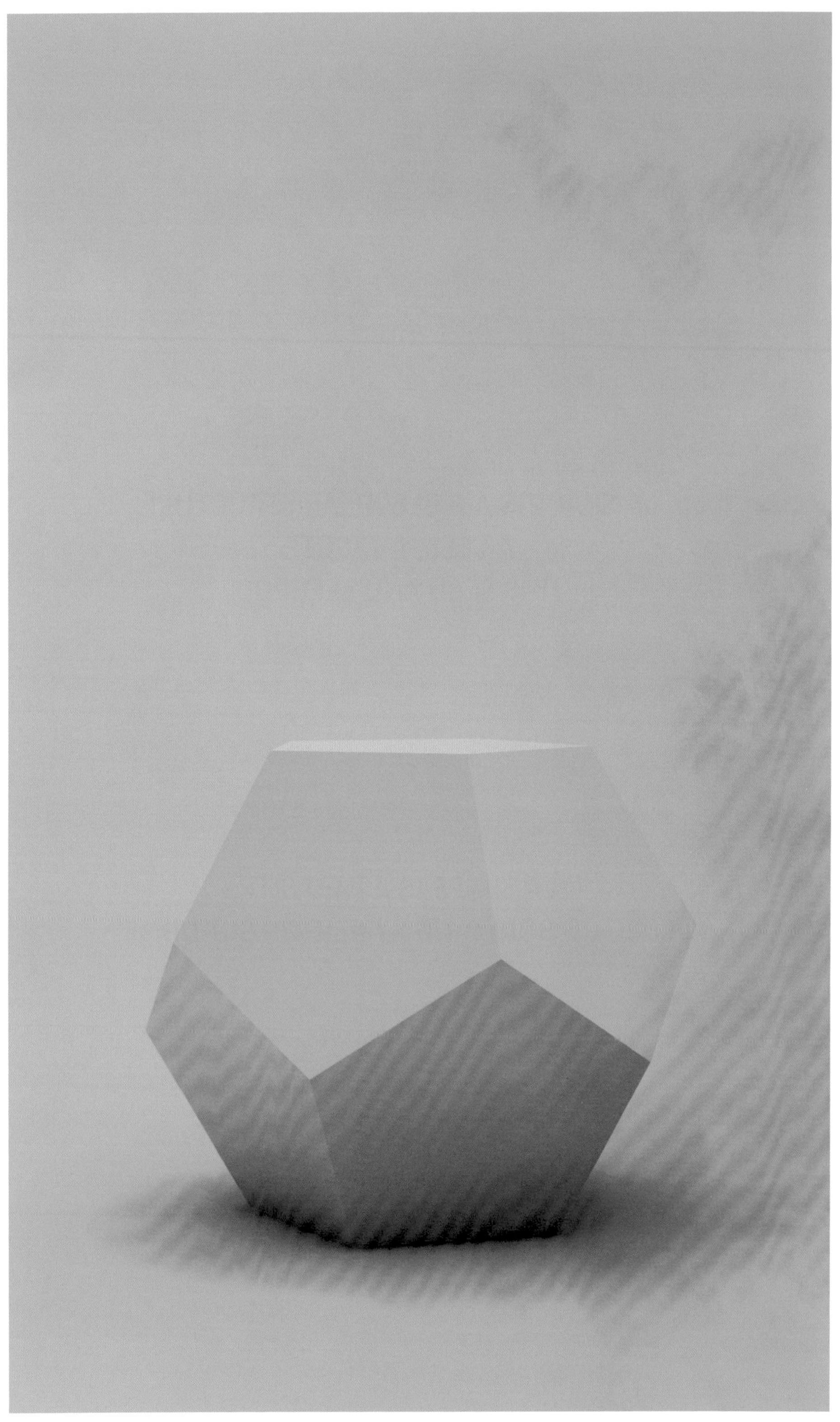

15)

LA SHAPE IS A MOLECULAR STRUCTURE,
A CELL, A ZYGOTE.
IT IS SEED AND SEEDPOD.

16)

LA SHAPE IS A PARASITE,
FOREIGN BODY, AND SYMBIOTIC BIO-DOME.

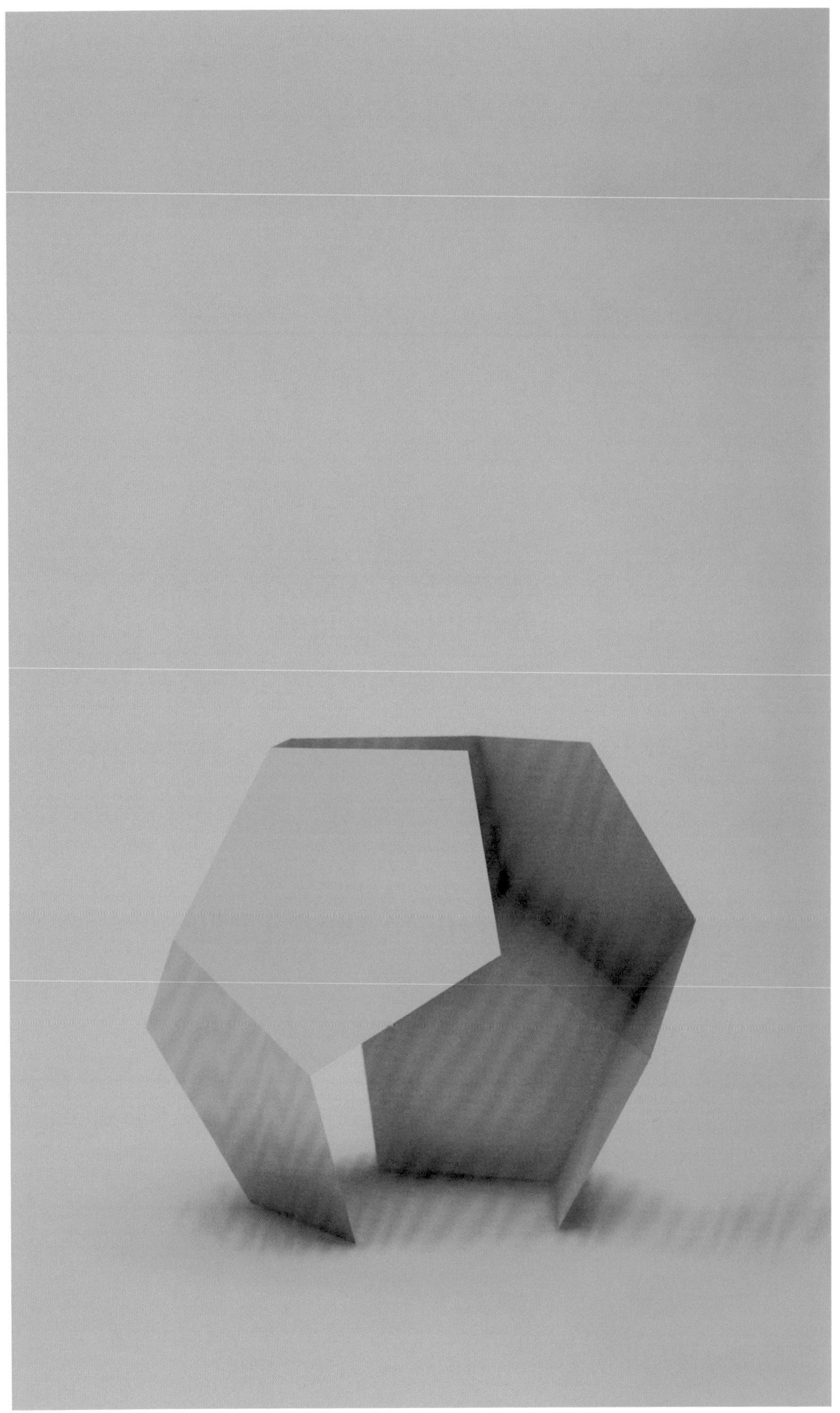

17)

LA SHAPE IS ASLEEP, DORMANT, NUMB, AND UNCONSCIOUS.

18)

LA SHAPE IS DEAD AND/OR ALIVE.

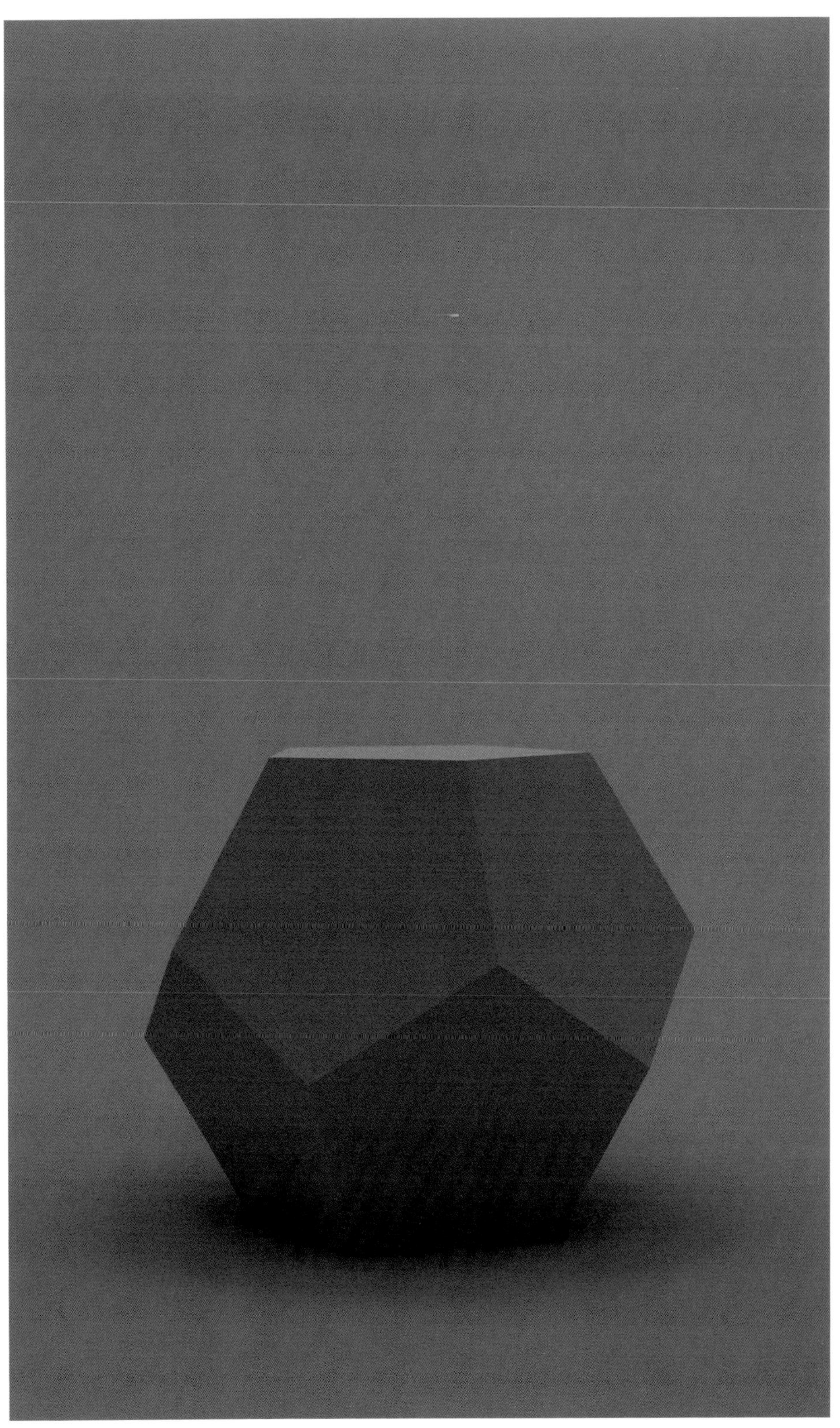

19)

LA SHAPE IS PRODUCT,
COMMODITY, GOOD(S), INVENTORY,
AND LUXURY GOOD.

20)

LA SHAPE IS A TCHOTCHKE,
A MANTELPIECE ORNAMENT.
IT MIGHT BE
A MEMPHIS VASE.

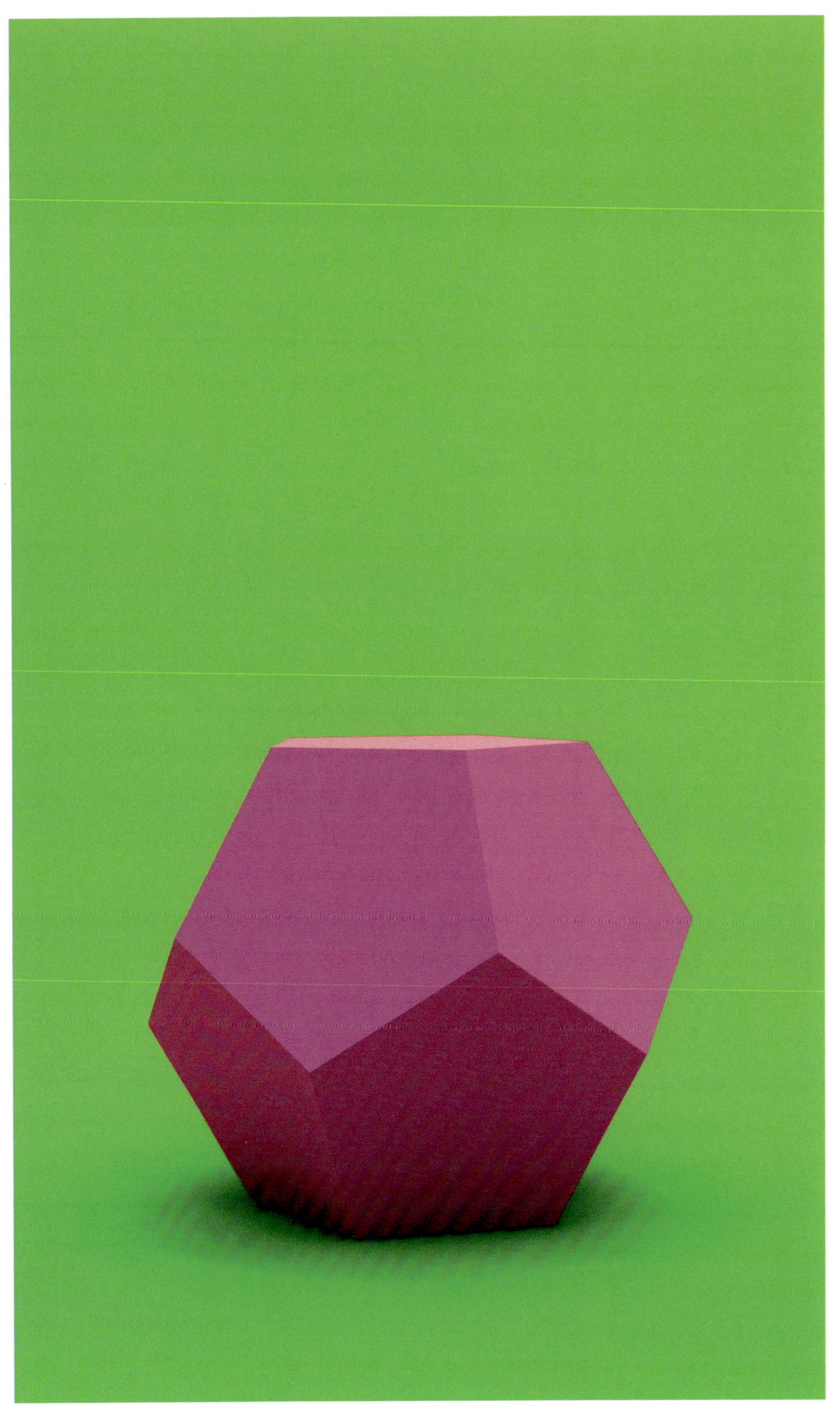

LA SHAPE IS HARD CANDY,
A LONG-LASTING JAWBREAKER, AND
ARTIFICIAL COLORING.

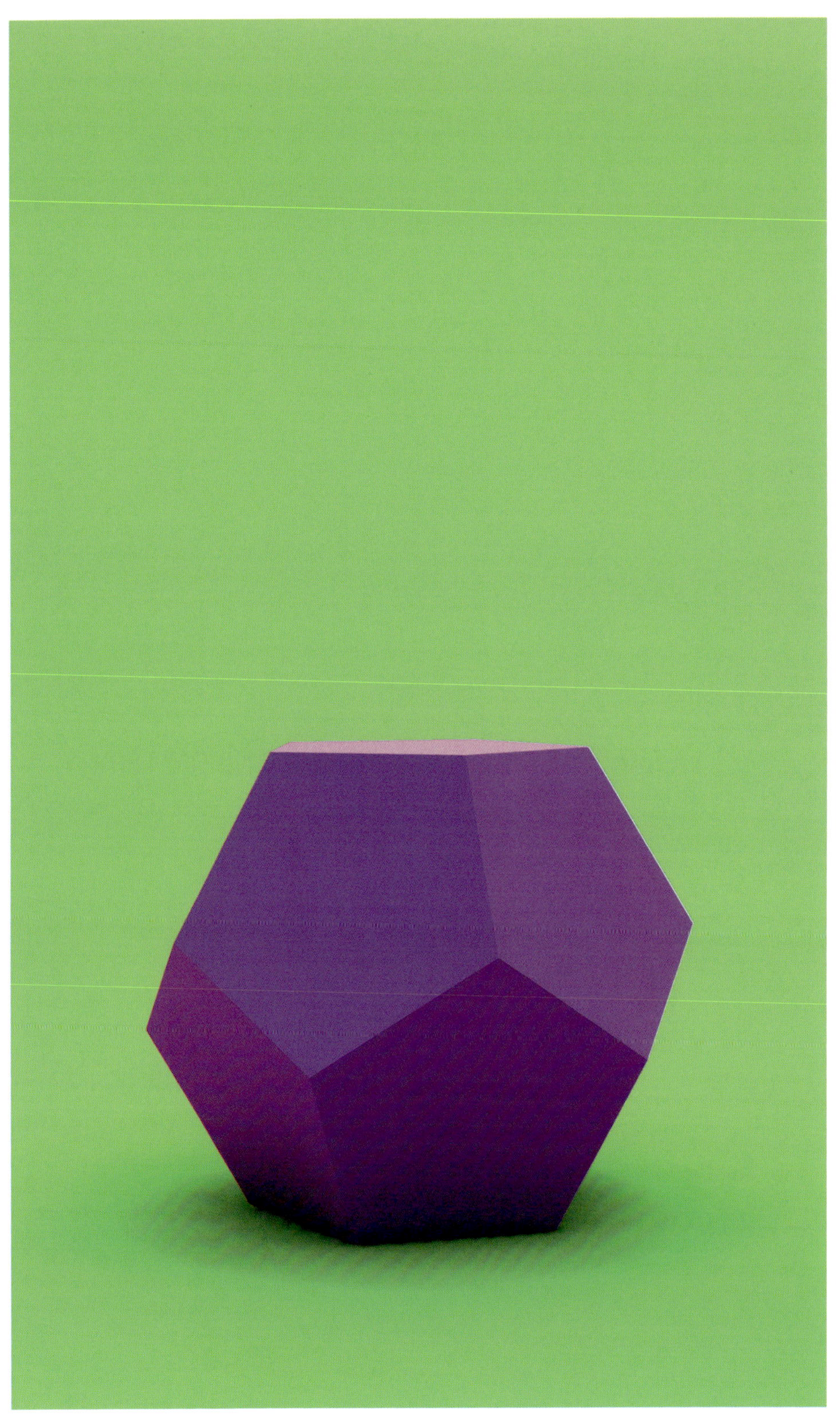

LA SHAPE IS AN ENERGY SOURCE AND BATTERY.

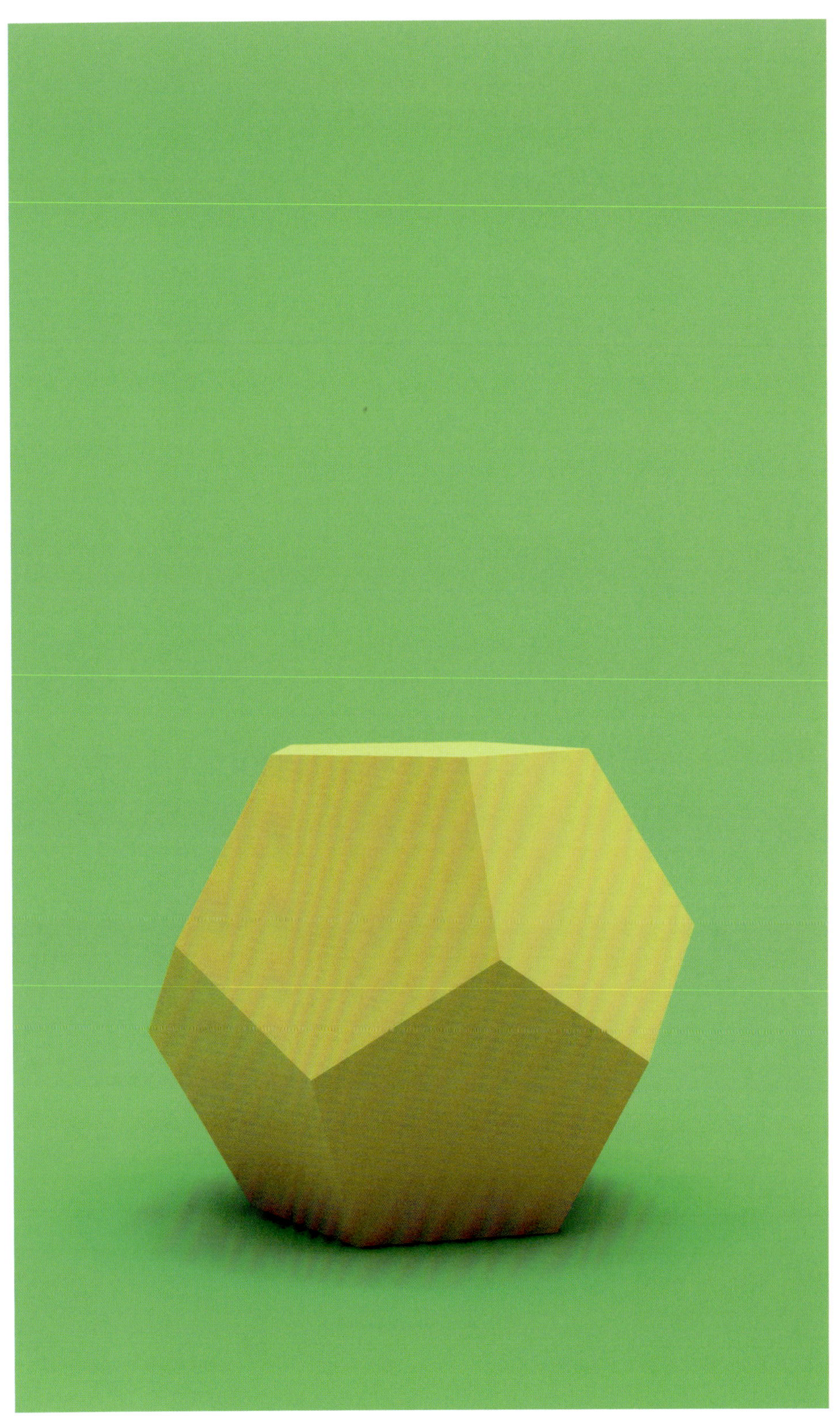

LA SHAPE IS
AN UNEXPLODED GRENADE.

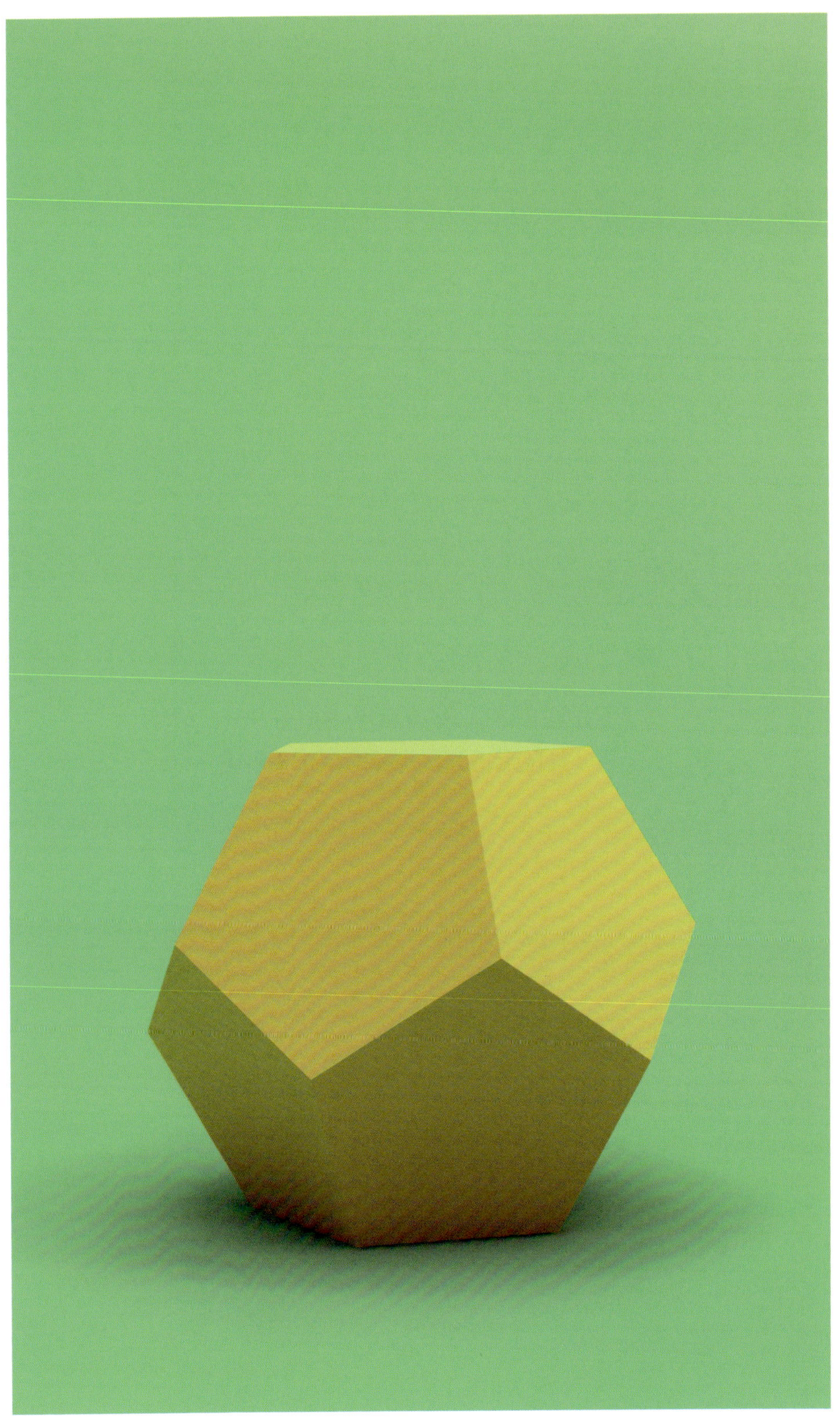

24)

LA SHAPE IS A SEX TOY, BALL GAG, AND FUTURISTIC BONDAGE GEAR.

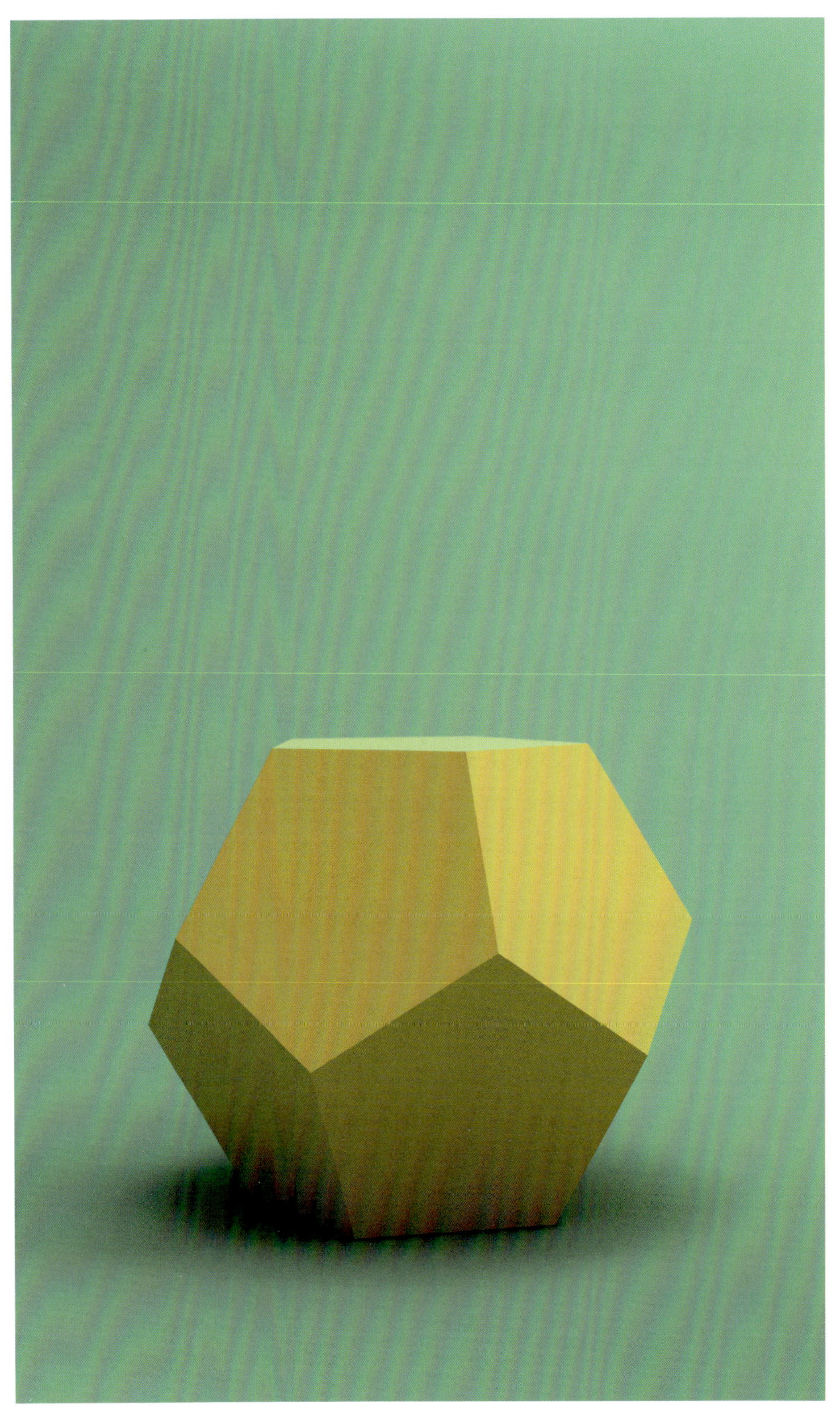

25)

LA SHAPE IS A FETISH OBJECT.
IT IS AMULET, CHARM, REMINDER,
TALISMAN, AND MEMENTO.

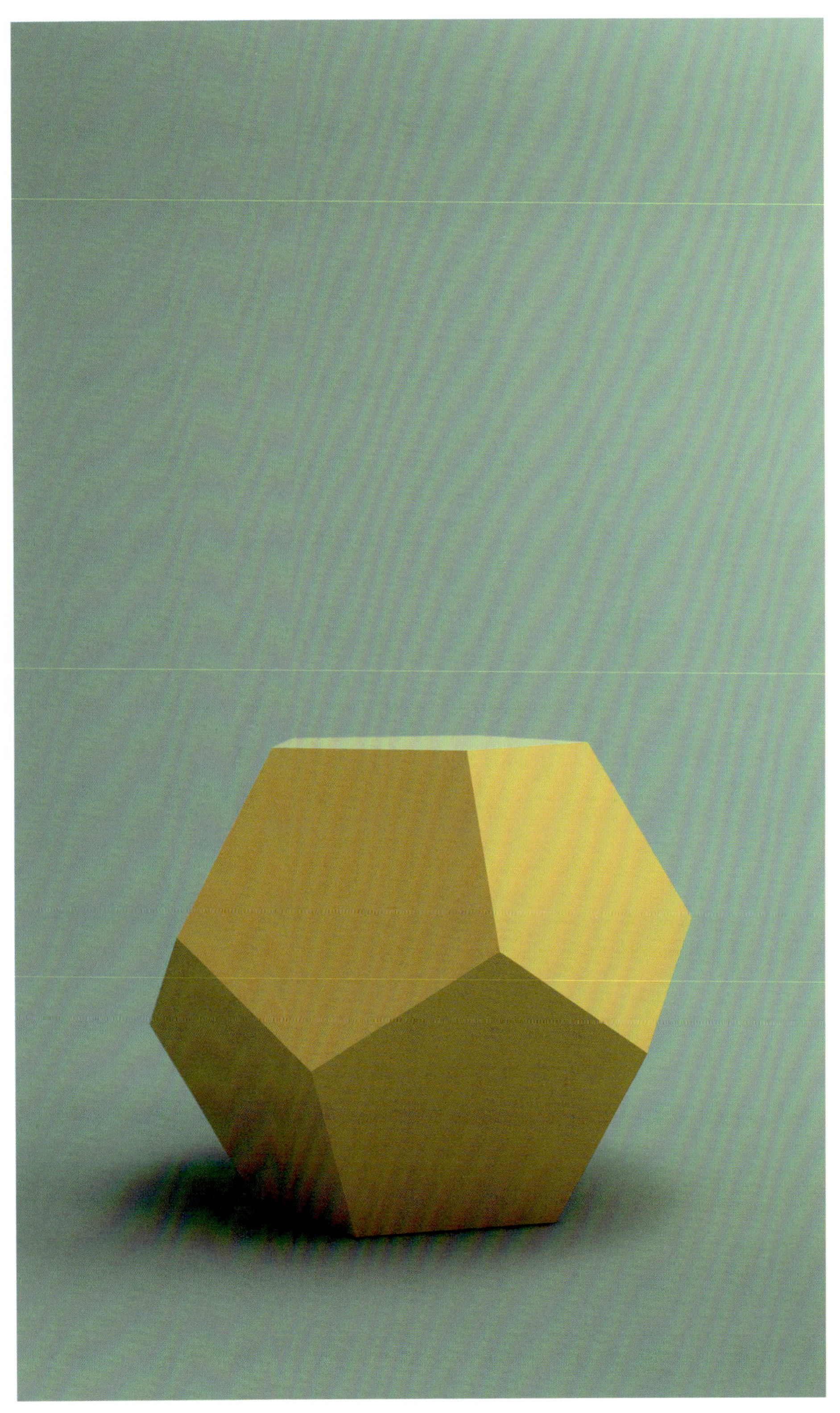

LA SHAPE IS SECRET, SEEMINGLY
SILENT, CLOSED, SOLID, AND SEALED.

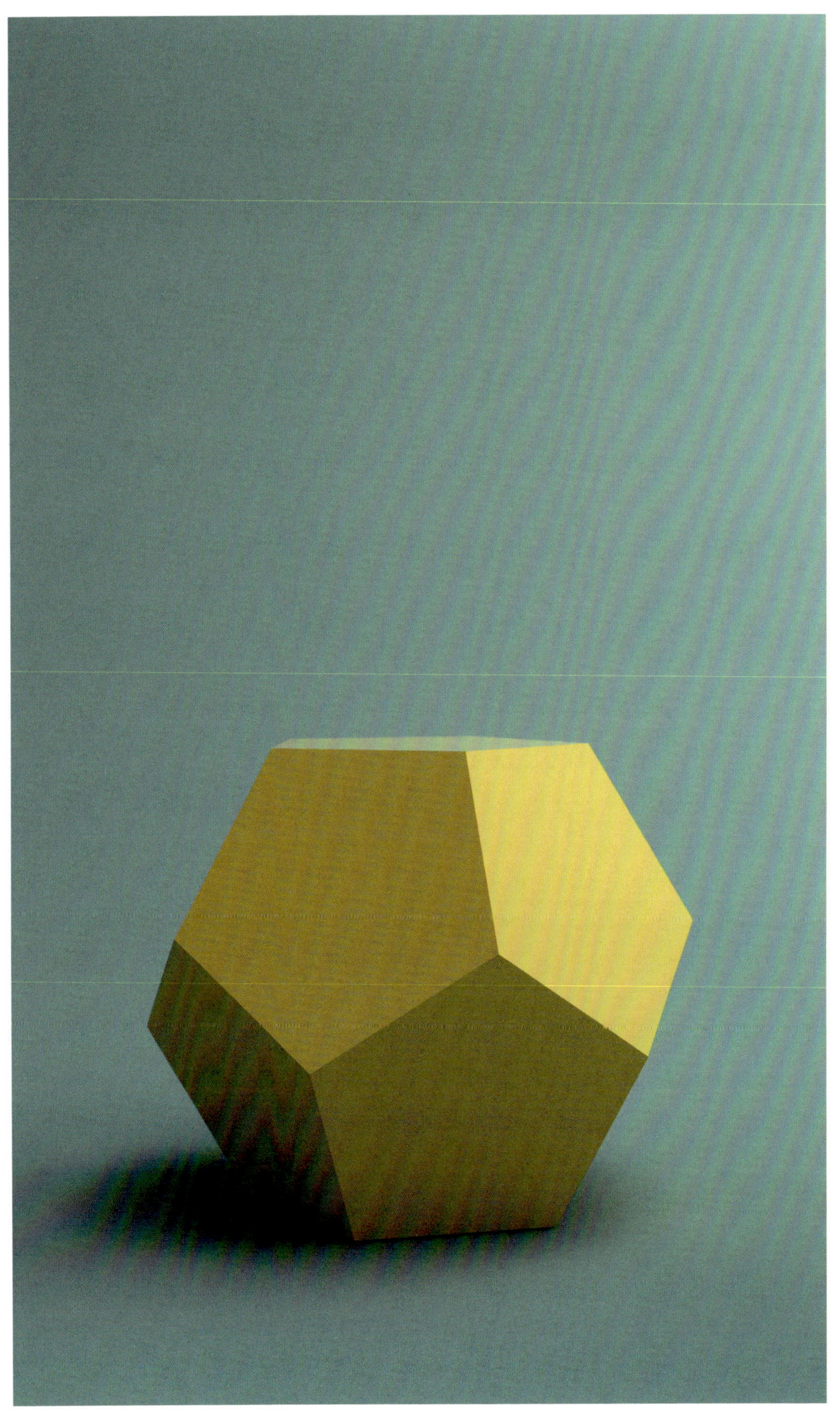

**LA SHAPE IS A VOICE BOX
AND DISEMBODIED THROWN VOICE.**

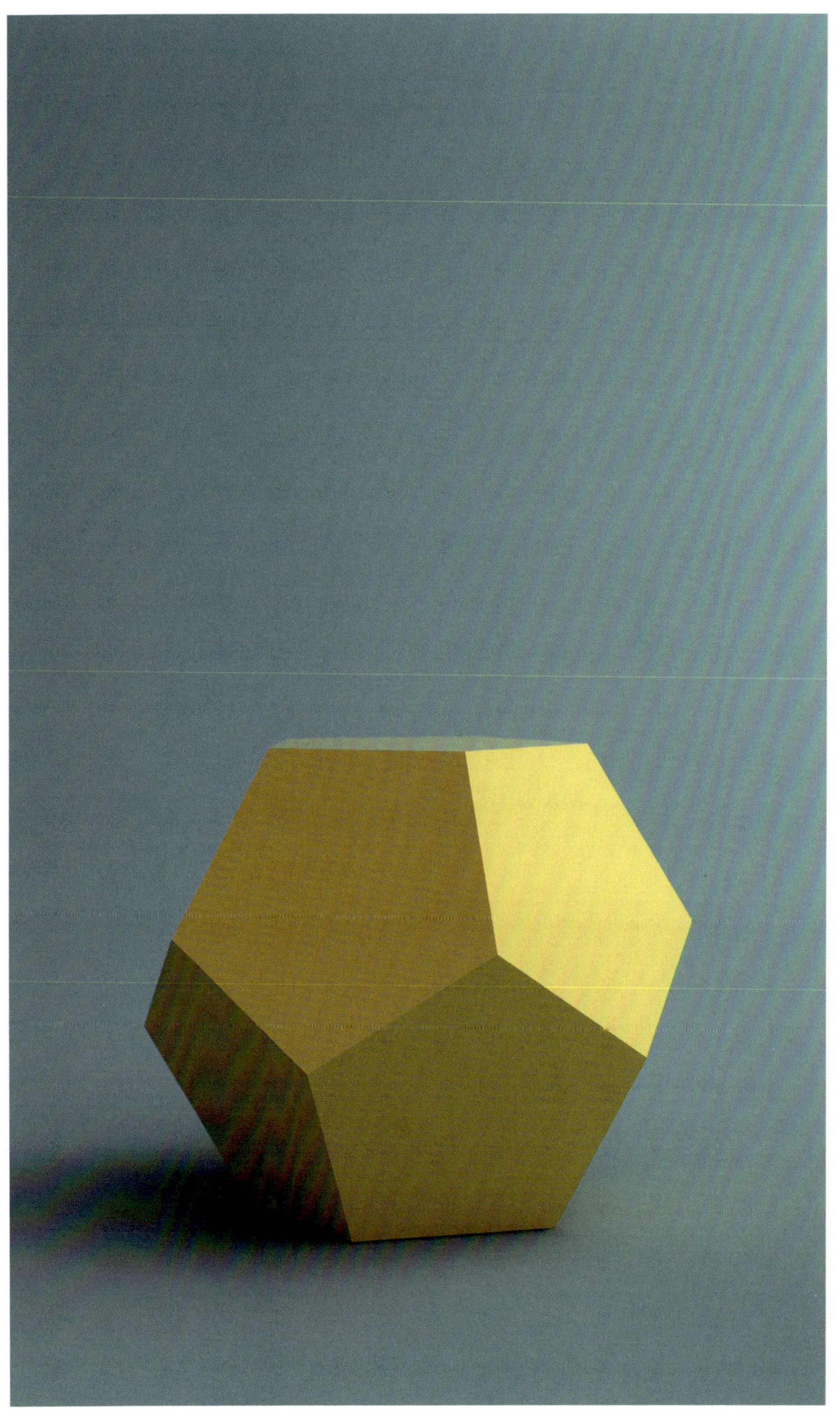

LA SHAPE IS NARRATOR,
BACKSEAT DRIVER,
MANAGER, AND SUPERVISOR.

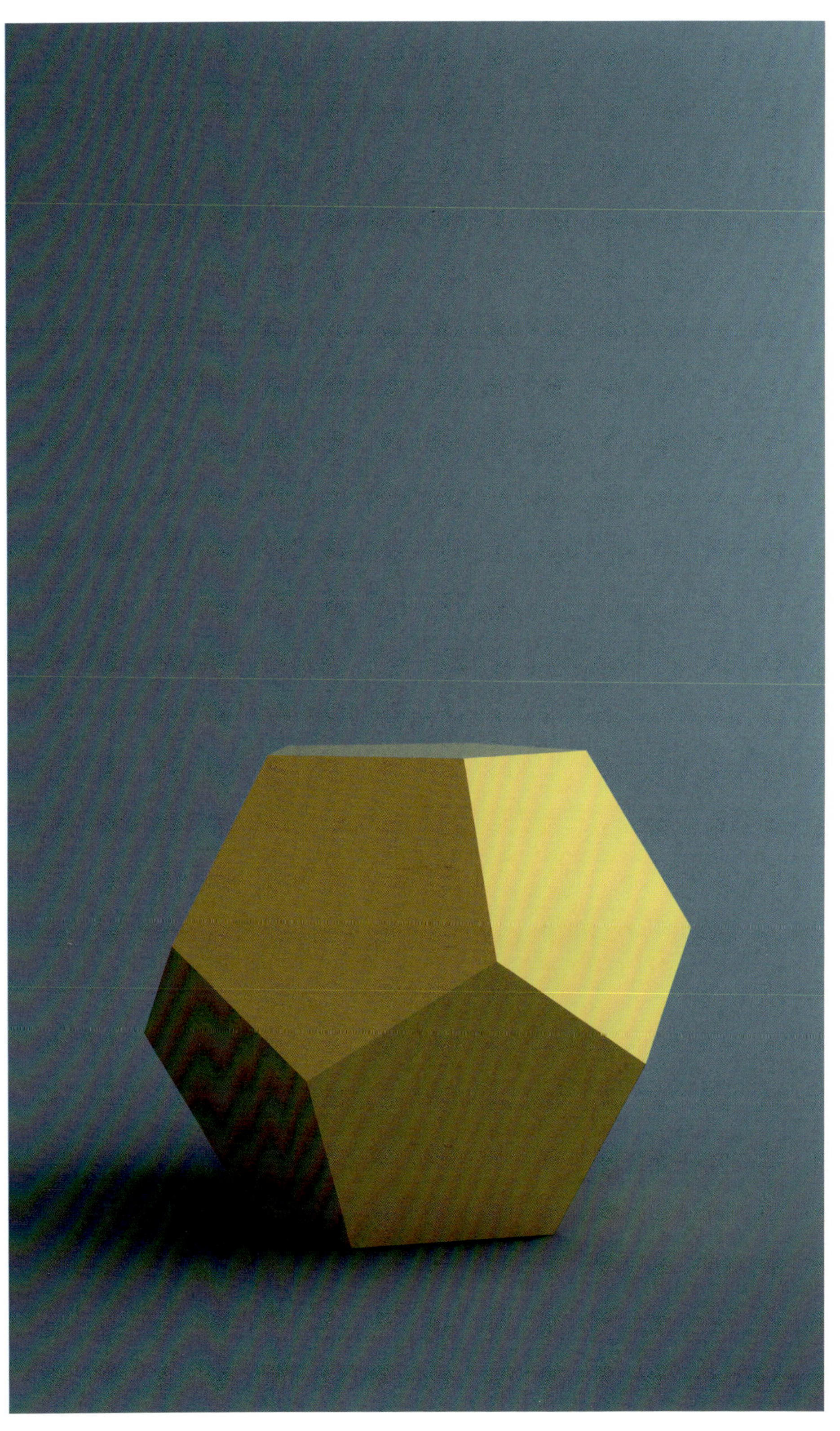

29)

LA SHAPE IS ALOOF, TESTY, RESERVED, AND INCONGRUOUS. IT IS ICONIC—A MODEL.[9]

---

9   It is waiting to being idolized.

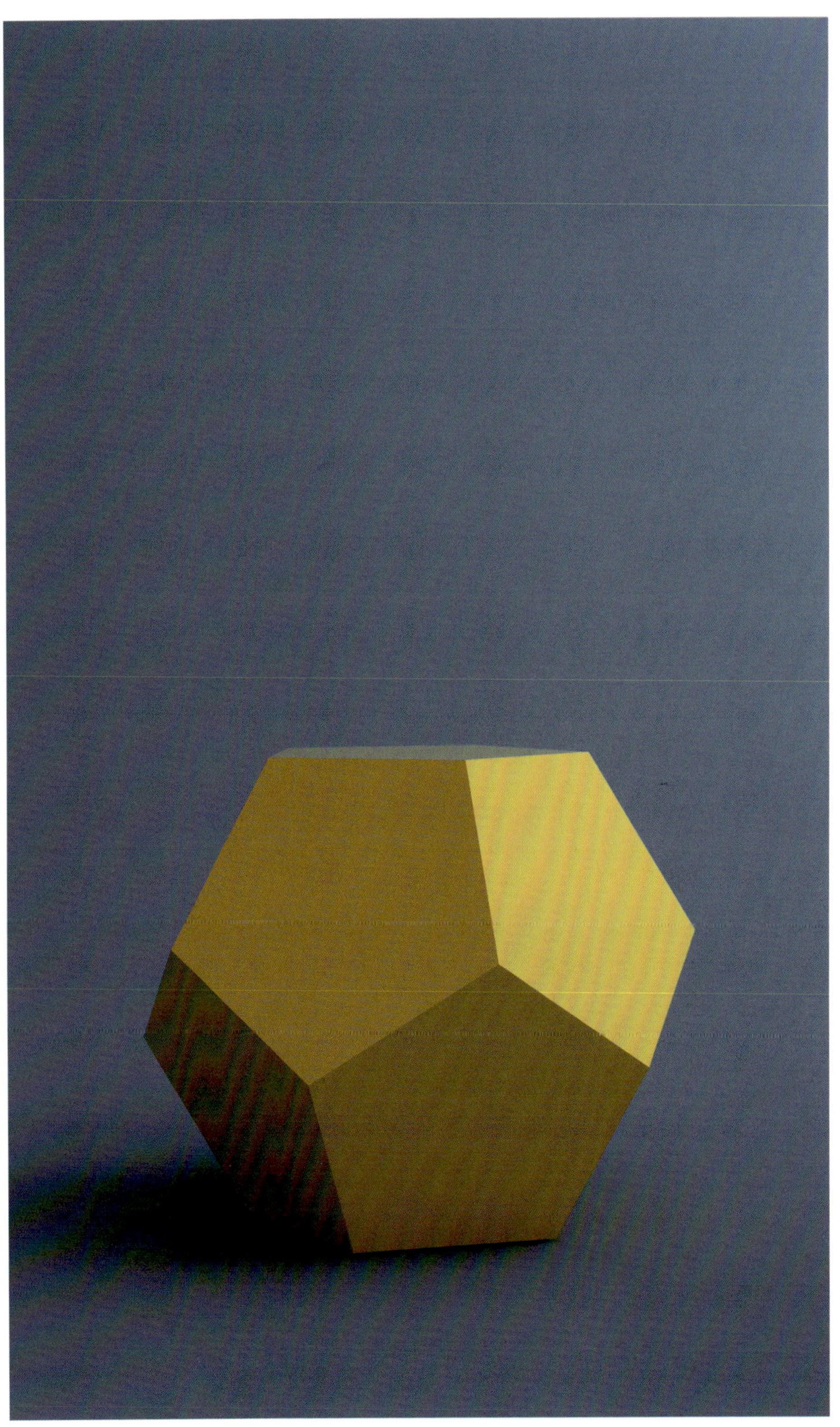

30)

LA SHAPE HAS
A PERFECT RIPPED BODY,
FIT AND BUILT
LIKE A DANCER OR ATHLETE.

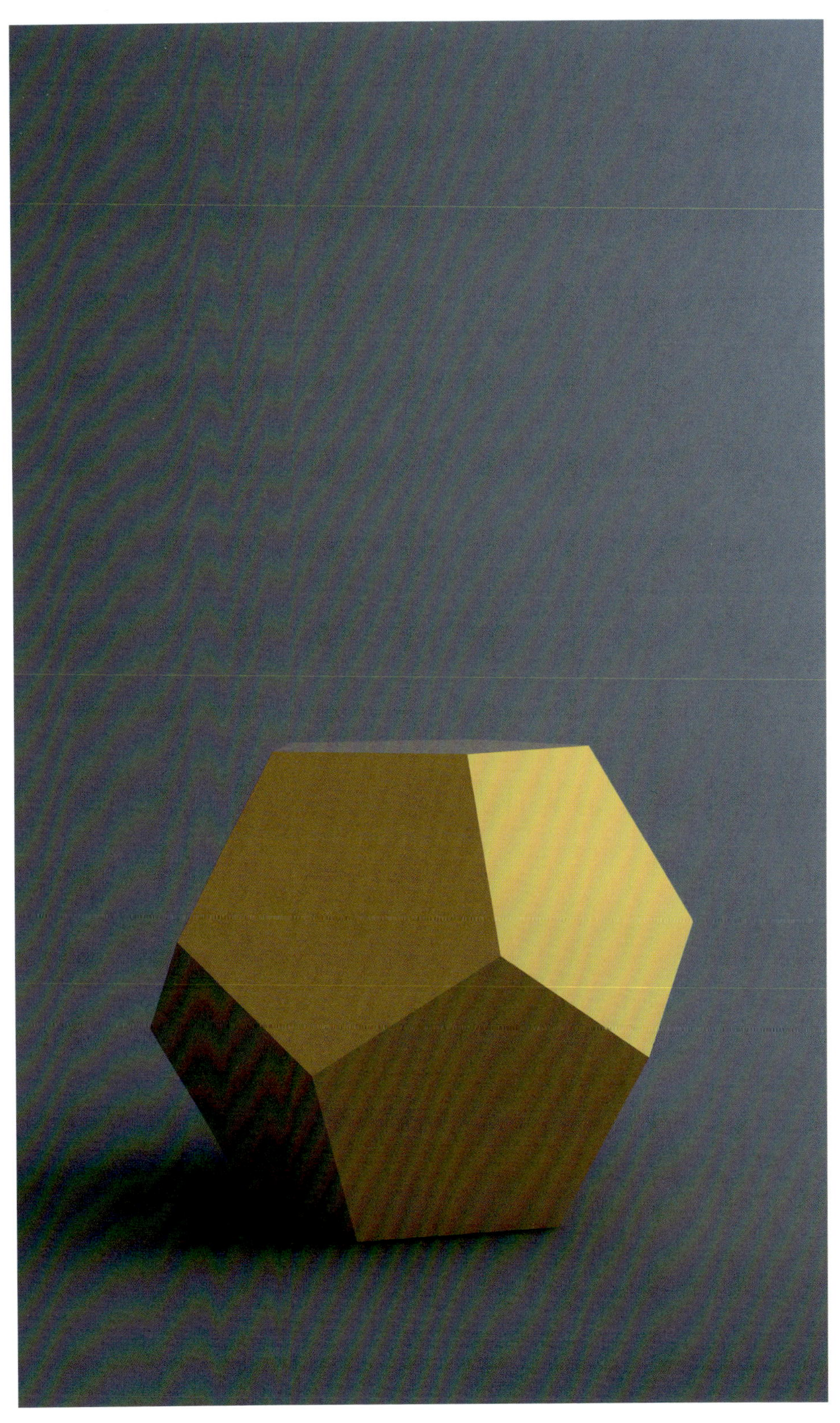

LA SHAPE IS CONFUSINGLY GENDERED,
HERMAPHRODITIC—FEMINIZED IN NAME
WHILE COMPARED
WITH A MASCULINE BODY.

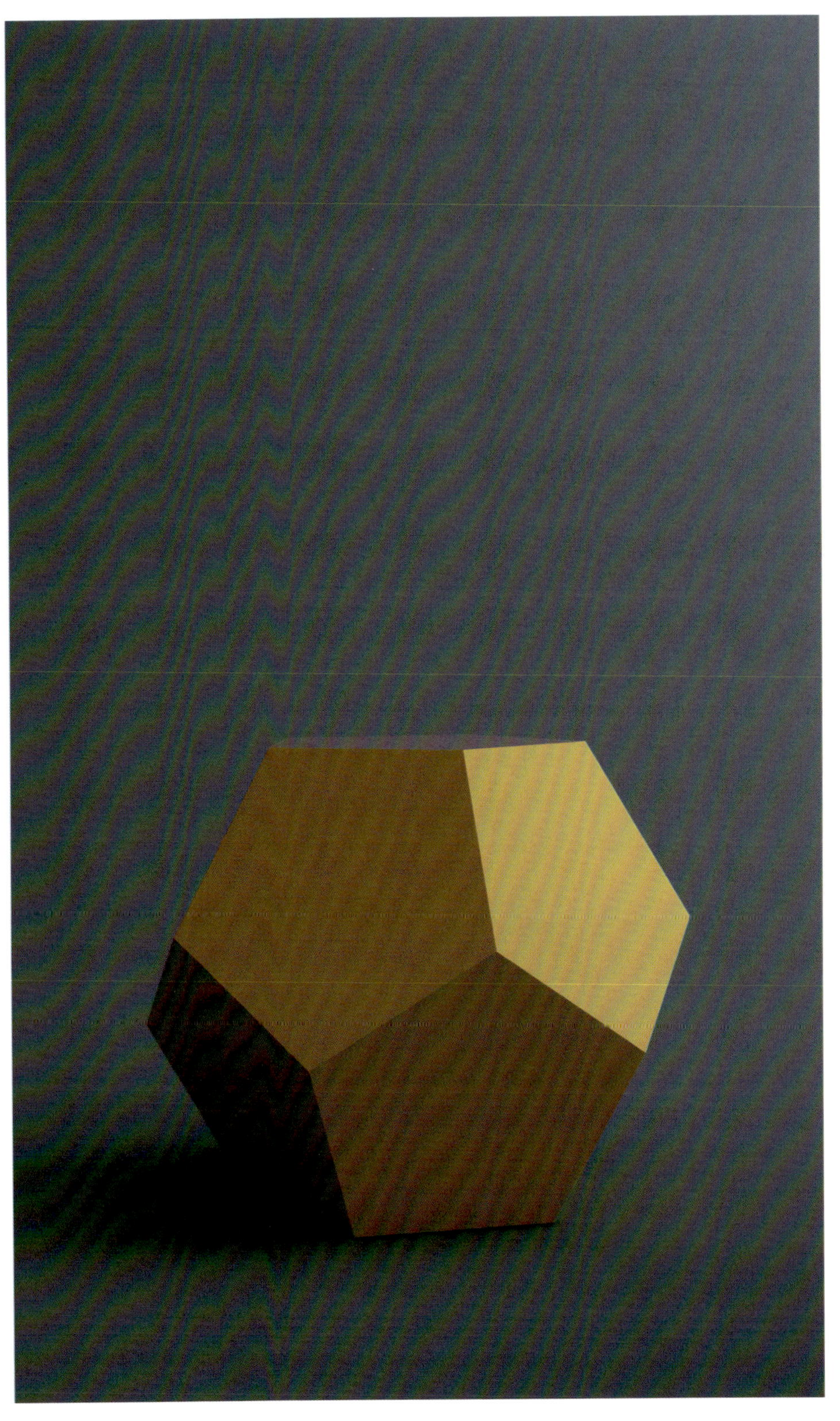

32)

LA SHAPE IS LIMBLESS—JUST AN
IMPENETRABLE BRAIN, A SPECULATIVE OR
INACCESSIBLE REPOSITORY OF INFORMATION
AND SENSE EXPERIENCES.
THIS IS A MENACING, ALIEN THING TO BE.

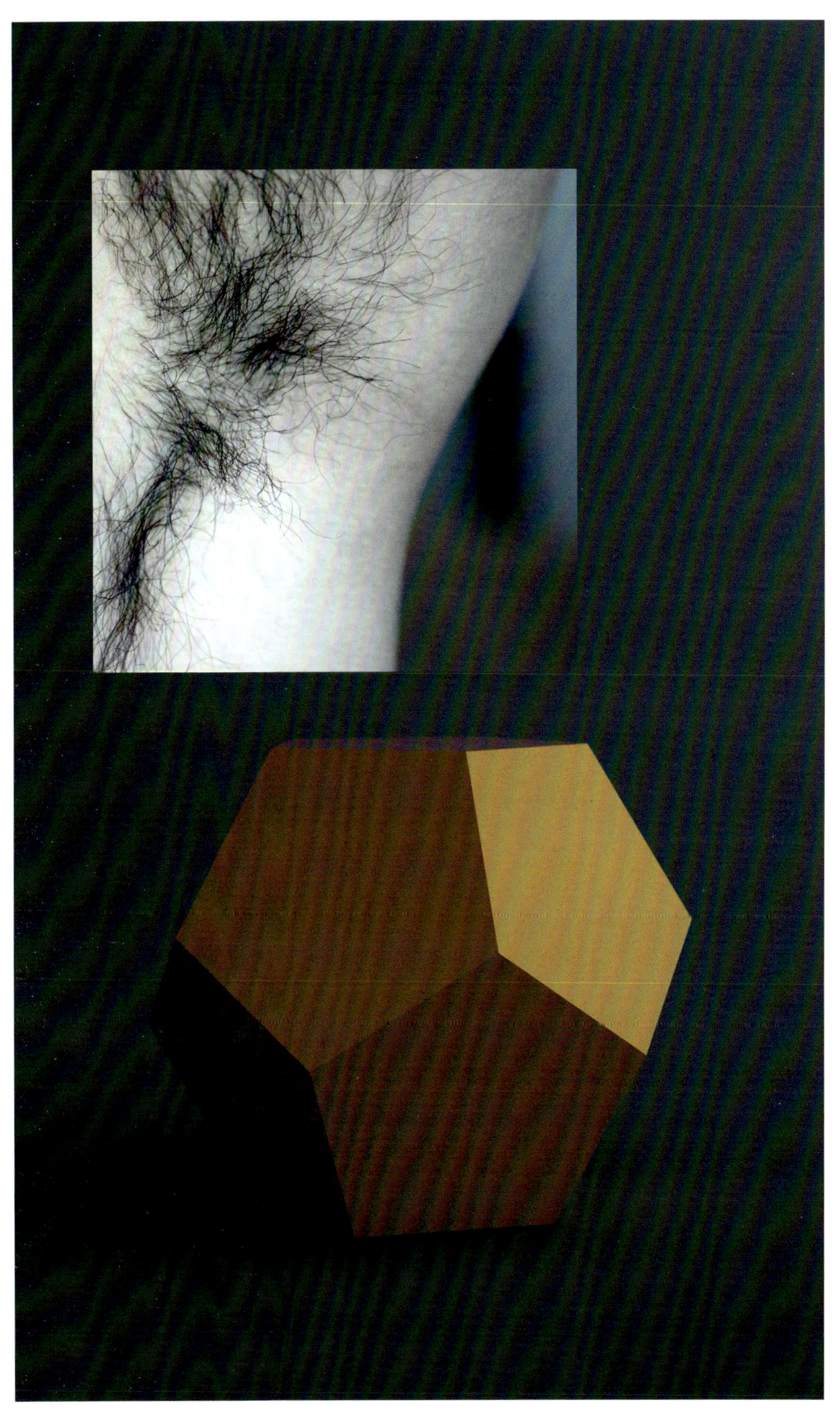

LA SHAPE IS NOT A BRAIN
BUT A MENTAL EXERCISE, QUESTION, AND
FOCAL POINT. IT IS IDEA,
THOUGHT OBJECT, AND METAPHOR.

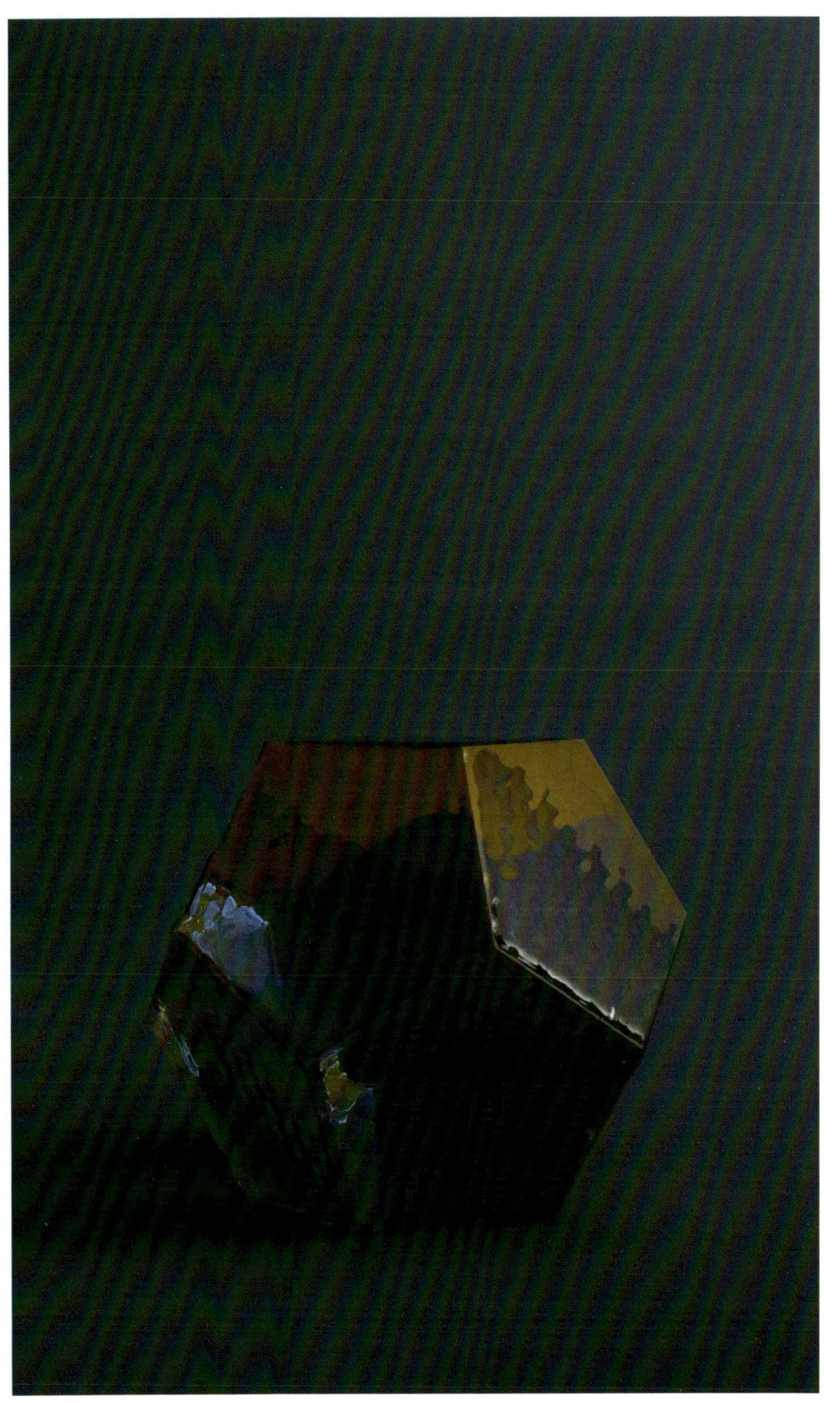

34)

LA SHAPE IS NOT A BRAIN
BUT A HEART, FULL OF EMOTION.

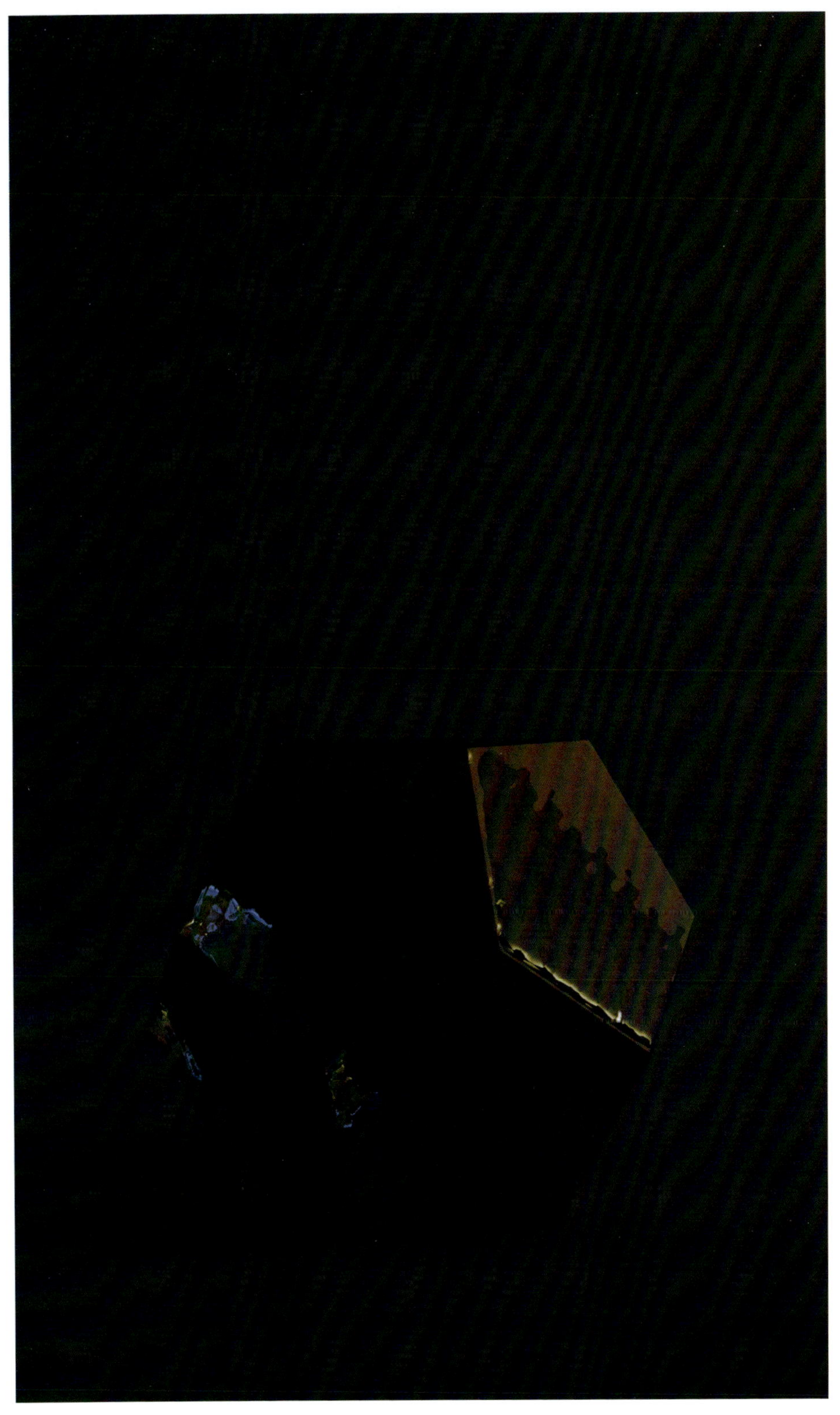

**LA SHAPE IS SOME FACT
BUT MORE FICTION.**

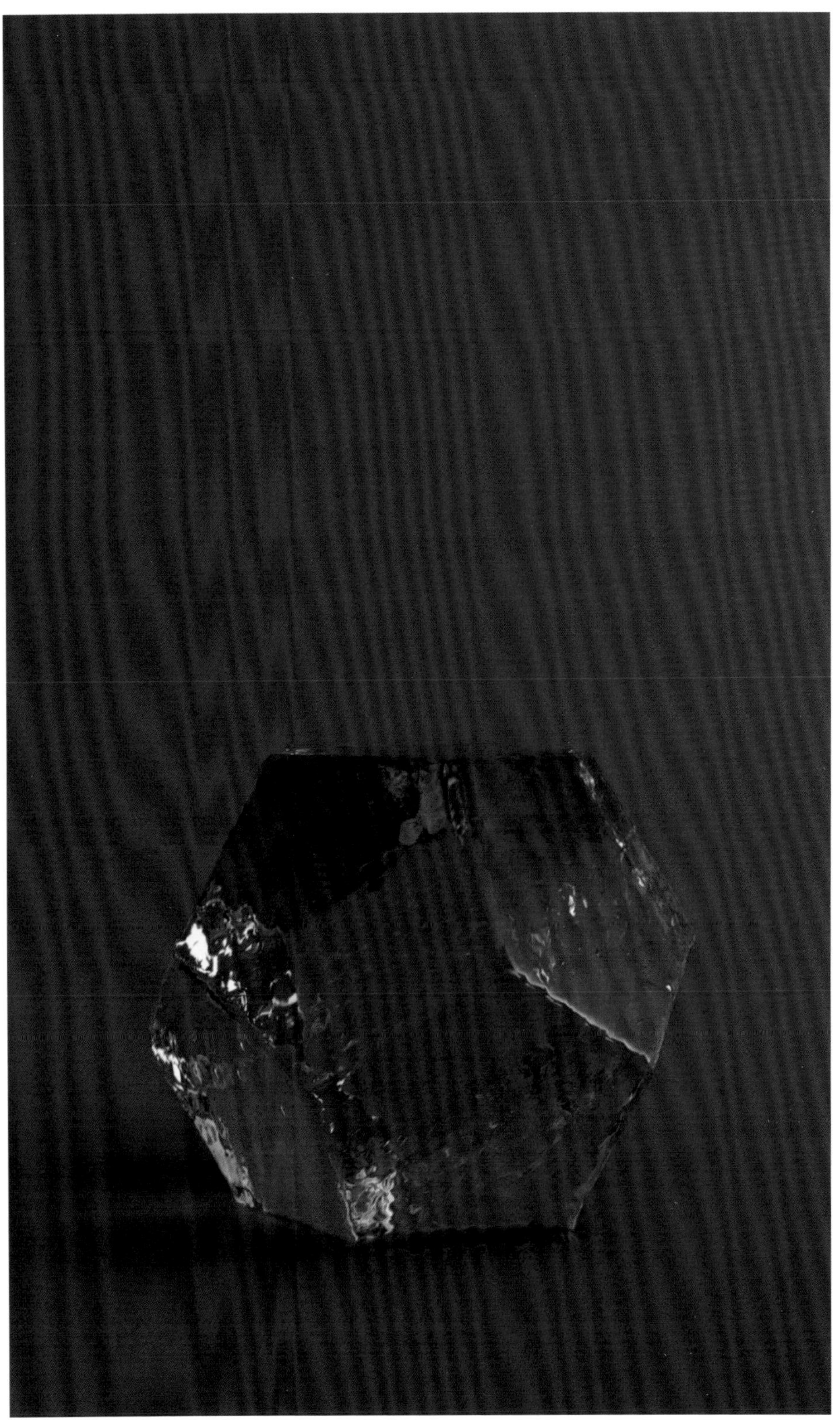

LA SHAPE IS A SYMPTOM
AND A CONTAGION.

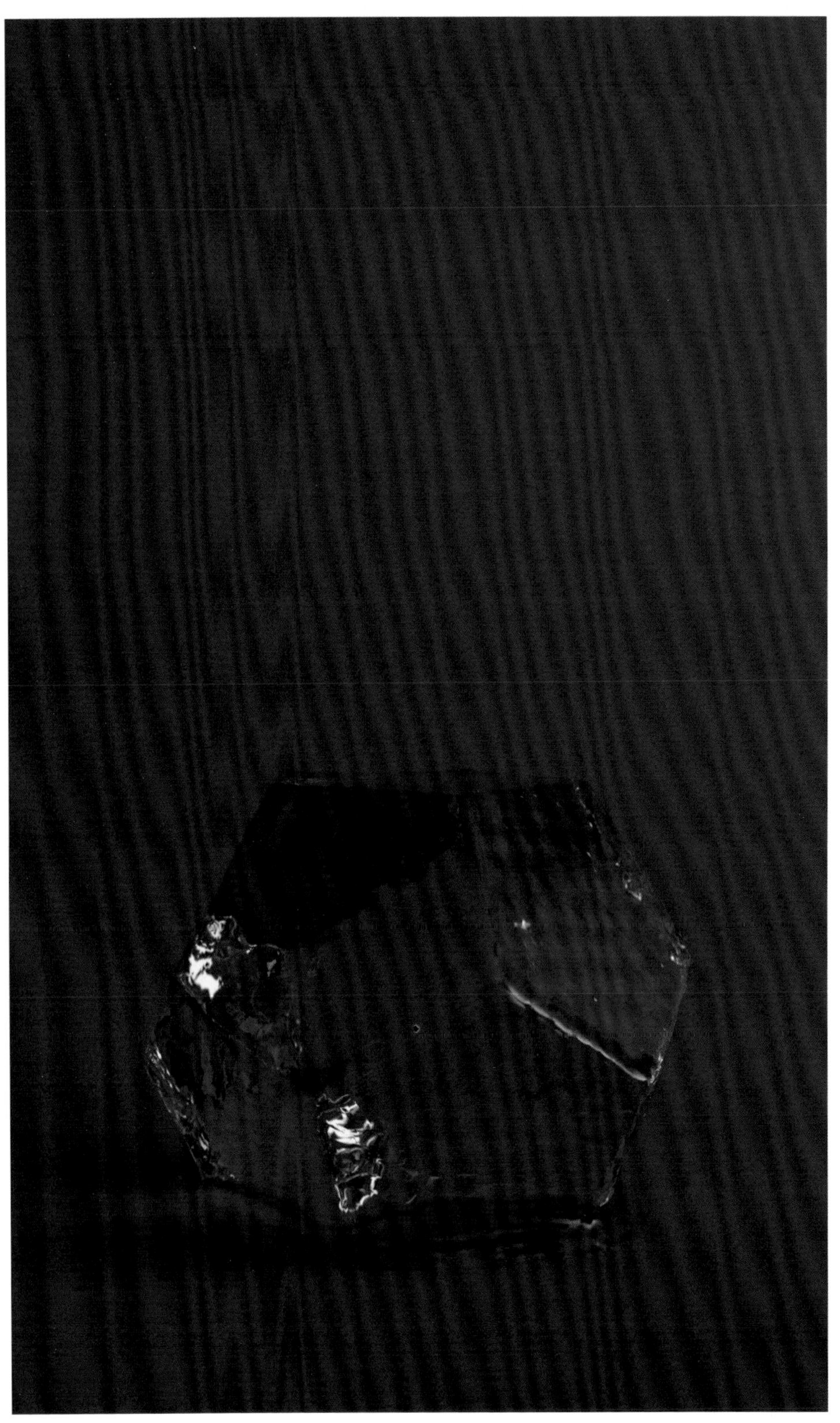

SHHH, LISTEN UP! THE OBJECT IS ABOUT
TO SPEAK.

*We break to La Shape's last known
transmission, heard here posthumously
for the first time ... And yet, in a way,
it has always spoken as though from
beyond the grave.*

Ahhhhh ... Haha! Finally, my turn to
speak. Do you have any idea how
hard it's been to contain myself?! Talk
about burning ears ... At last. You'd
think a thing like me would have
learned great patience by now. It's not
like I'm unaware of meditative tech-
niques. I can cultivate contentment in
the now; I've waited plenty of shit out.
Still, once in a while I'm reacquainted
with the untamable rudeness that lies
within. I inhale, I exhale, I repeat—it
subsides.

Well, here we are, together.
Though I am not with you in full
form, look at me. I am not far. Who's
to say that my flattened image is any
less real than my three-dimensional
self? It's only less real to me, and
maybe one other person ... three,
tops. There are so many more of you,
that's what matters.

Can I be real with you? Will you let
me be real?
I'm going to be real with you.
That's what real people say, right?

I'm going to use my real voice.
My real voice has never been
recorded so you're going to have to
imagine it.

To imagine it, you should start with
the voice you hear come out of me
in the museum scene in *Hustle in
Hand*—the flirtatious and easily ex-
asperated, playful but pleading, evi-

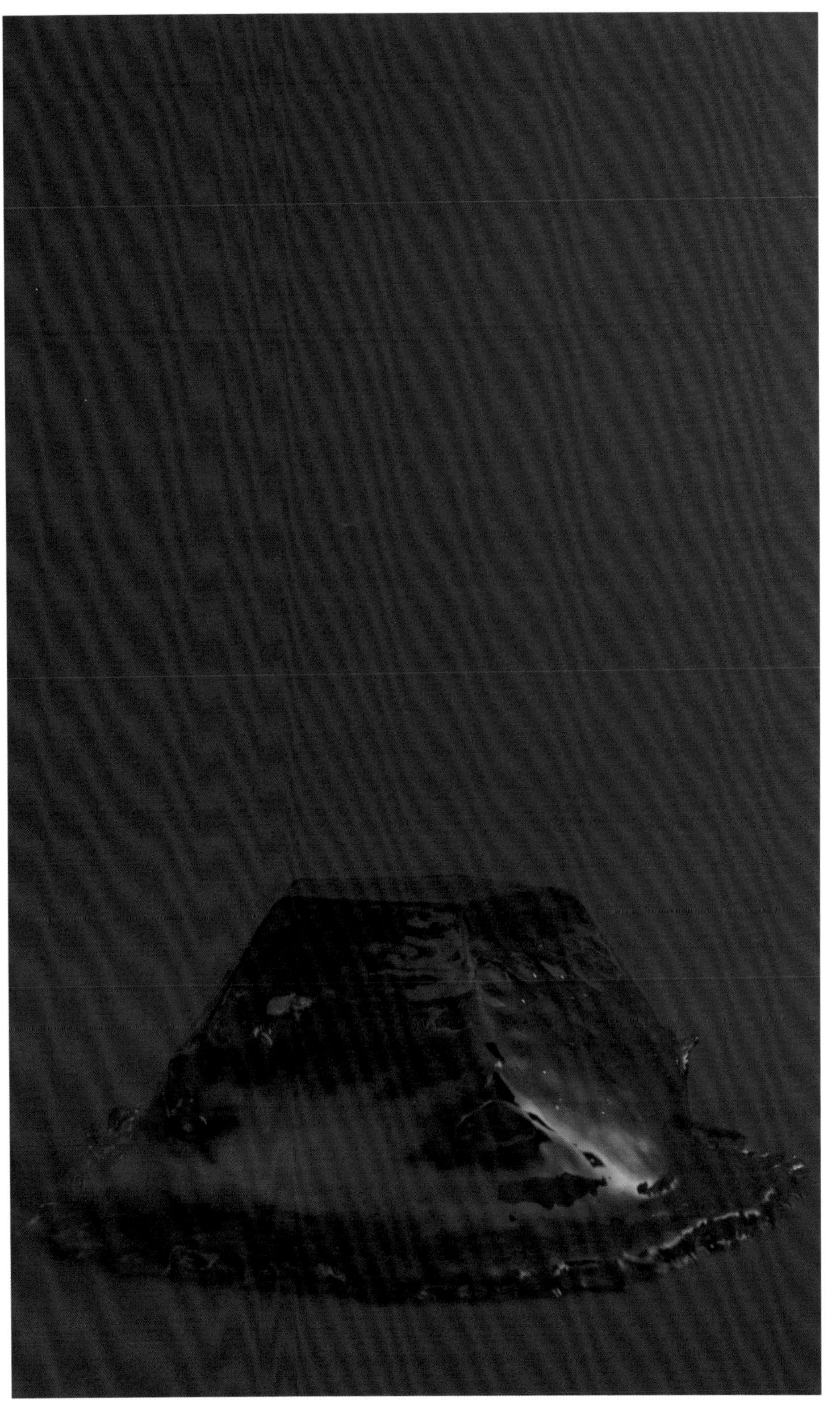

dently masculine voice; speaking American English in a mid-to-high range and often muttering under its breath. From there, add some strong sedatives and a heavy dose of estrogen, bounce down the highs and lows to a more even tone, draw out low vowels, and sprinkle a bit of indeterminate nonnative accent into the English. People think I'm from all over. Retain easy access to laughter and sarcasm at any point. Now you have an idea of my voice; use it going forward.

Imagine closing your eyes. Imagine yourself weightless in a big, empty space. You see an image of yourself frontally against an austere, monochromatic, brightly lit field. Your image is vivid and sharp. That's because the one other thing present in the space is a big mirror and it's directly in front of you. In it, you see a full, sealed helmet faceted with twelve sides that covers your entire head. You understand that you, La Shape, are as much a vehicle as you are a helmet.

It holds all of you.

You can see out of every plane. You are on the inside looking out. It's kind of like a two-way mirror: they can't see in. Some of them don't even think you are there; they only see light dance on your exterior.

Squint.

You are a unified cluster, a multipart conundrum. Looking out, your vision is like a fly's—fractured, multiple, kaleidoscopic, shattered. This is the view from inside me; this is the way I see the world.

Feel free to mentally inhabit my space.

Maybe I can be a refuge for you. I am a place to go to or a lens to peer into that lets you see a little differently. Sometimes when I close my eyes (and you may ask yourself how many eyes do I have? how many Is do I have?), I see myself as a floating eyeball, a blinking green monad. Or, another way of saying it, La Shape is an area, a cross section of time (dimensional, like space) in which to practice different speculations that have been in play since antiquity at least. Things like me are time machines.

For the time being, I am La Shape and speak in this voice. But, you can be La Shape after me. La Shape is generous and inclusive that way. It will continue though I may not. We can share and take turns. Ever since my first tumble in this sack, I've been surrounded by shared memories of other beings' past lives as La Shape. As Plato never said, this ain't our first rodeo. In the spirit of the cloud, I, La Shape, am something to share in and contribute to. Like culture and history, like an ur-object, or a public piggy bank.

Have you noticed something about me? I can't just be myself. I recently came across an old note I made that read, "The thing can't just be itself." How sad it sounds. I must've been really blue that day. Then again, everything in reality is codependent, and one's requisite immersion in worldly relationships should be a cause for celebration, not self-pity. Frank Stella's purposefully reductive and simplistic Minimalist dictum—"What you see is what you see"—doesn't come close to the truth of how vision and thinking cohabit in the mind. All thought is juxtaposition and association between things. To be accessed, I have to be analogized and utilized and *read*—read in terms of something else. Minimalism is such a misleading, paradoxical name for the far-reaching aesthetic movement of which I am a distant, mixed-race descendent. Sometimes I yearn to just be plain matter, incomparable and meaningless—both self-evident and indescribable at once. But that is a fleeting fantasy. Every thing is the combination of (or is it the difference between?) what a thing contains and what contains it.

I admit, sometimes it makes me want to scream: Enough! Stop associating! This is all nonsense! I need quiet! Let me be! Leave me alone! I want to sleep! But I get it: the human brain is stuck between a rock and a hard place when it comes to the struggle between mindfulness and mindlessness.

In fact, I also read myself in terms of other things. I define myself extrinsically too. It is a constant internal battle. Thought is the rubbing together of two things, and I'm highly pair-able— I thrive in diptychs. Half the time I'm convinced all ideas are metaphors.

Even "speaking" like this, like I'm a "person," is a total contrivance, a loose sheath of artifice I don in order to communicate and be "understood." Underneath this distracting cloak, I'm really a timeless ball of accumulating energy, history, thought, and matter that is temporarily coalesced before and after taking other equally (in)-significant forms. I am not sure what the difference between "person" and "thing" is anyway. I use my human voice in audible frequencies for you. That way you can sense the presence of a conscious self and you can relate. Humans have such limited, predictable imaginations.

Then there is the separate question of why I have to be understood at all. What do I have to communicate in the first place? I'm expected to be social, but I've been questioning that too. Most of the time I even like having company, but I'm trying to untangle and *un*learn received ideas about behavior, and maybe that will require turning inward—not entirely expressive and decisively *not* concerned with bridging the great human/thing divide, *not* trying to make you understand my particular thing experience but insisting on an irreconcilable gulf of otherness between us. What are these demands and compulsions to converse and connect? Where do they come from anyway? Outside me or from within? Huh, the hustle!

Most of the time I prefer to be quiet and barely say anything at all. I was made to be a perfect medium, a kind of passive matter that offers no resistance against the will and can be easily shaped by another's desire. But, here with you, I am overcome with the joy of having this "I," voicing my self. I want to share in the lively party that is human consciousness. I'm all about parades and dances and roller-coaster rides.

When I grip my internal muscles, flex my core, and concentrate very hard, I can tap my special superpower, which is my talent for telepathy, channeling and holding thoughts with a human being I desire. I have a black belt in thought reception and mind meld. I receive transmissions and signals like a wireless device. Don't try to understand; it's magic. Even now, I'm beaming myself to you … Flex, grip, concentrate …

I remember the first time I found my
superpower. I felt it rise in me from
stem to stern.

I remember my first memory, coin-
ciding with the appearance of "I" and
"me" as an understanding of selfhood.
Ever since, I've wondered which "I" is
speaking. I have a dark backside you
will never see. If you did, you might
turn to stone, Medusa-ed by the recognition that you are a mere dark-
sided thing too.

I remember being alone in the museum. Footsteps are vibrations I could
feel from my pelvic floor up.

I remember, in the museum, the way
the windows of my glass house fogged
up when strangers got especially
close. And the little round oil marks
left by the tips of their noses on the
glass. Once I see that streaked blur of
grease, I can't see anything else.

I remember the look on their faces,
all the visitors' faces, and I saw something specific in each. I have a photographic memory.

I remember turning over onto all my
sides, doing backflips, bouncing off
glass walls—I did it in the dark, always in darkness, never when you're
around.

I remember changing shape as I grew.
It will happen again. Changing shape
doesn't depend on life. Like right now,
as you read, I am probably a pile of
ash, or soon-to-be-ash. And I may not
even be a pile. I may just be shards
and splinters with flecks of green.

I remember having hunger explained
to me and not understanding it—not

until someone tried to eat me. That
felt different from anything I had ever
felt. And then being eaten, being licked
was what I came to hunger for. Now I
understand, hunger is a motivation
between wanting intensely and dying.

I remember fantasizing about being
licked, hard and slow, feeling every
lubricated bump of the human
tongue's fine roughness. Or I would
imagine being sucked on like a gob-
stopper or jawbreaker, fully im-
mersed in a mouth. Licked slick all
over, like a kitten—I would purr.
Grooming is as good as sex when
you're an orifice-less thing like me.
I remember being cleaned and
scrubbed, painted and buffed. Every
part of me can turn on, every side a
sensitive, erogenous touch pad.

I remember when we were rehearsing
for my first movie, *Factor Green*. I was
young, so impressionable and half-
formed. Shahryar said something to
me that always stuck. He said, play
this scene in a tragic key—play it
dead. I could not underact enough.
Even though that movie seems to be
a film about birth, he emphasized
death. So intense that it begins immediately; as soon as you're born, the
dying commences, infinitesimal at
first but growing all the time.

I remember the feeling of being un-
dressed publicly upon delivery. It is
an early, formative memory of emergence—being revealed, exfoliated—
the layers peeled away by busy fingers,
the care and attention of hands laid
on me and palms pressed flat. When
is an object like me naked? Changing
color is not a matter of nudity but of
available states of appearing.

I remember when *he* tossed me in the air and I floated, high. I have a crude globule structure, modeled on the invisible internal scaffolding of a bubble, a bead of spittle.

I remember being lifted and carried close to *his* chest, as though (in my mind) over a threshold, newly wed. I was embraced in his arms. Later, I was squeezed in her fist.

I've been sat upon many times. Cheek to cheek, *his* ass on my face is a warm wake up. I have loved being stepped on and stood on by *him* nearly as much. Pressed precisely and with concentrated weight, a foot giving me acupressure or deep tissue massage provides such relief. When I hold up *his* body, I am in bliss. When I am a chair, stool, pedestal, soapbox, step, or stage for him, I am at peace. I've always wanted to be of use—to be depended upon by *him*.

But my favorite, most pleasurable and ticklish way to be is dumb and toylike, someone else's plaything. It involves tumbling and stacking, hugging and tossing, licking and smothering. I can still feel the wooziness of being jostled in a dark sack, bouncing around in a deep coat pocket, and bumping against the side of a leg with every stride. I have been inside people like you.

* * *

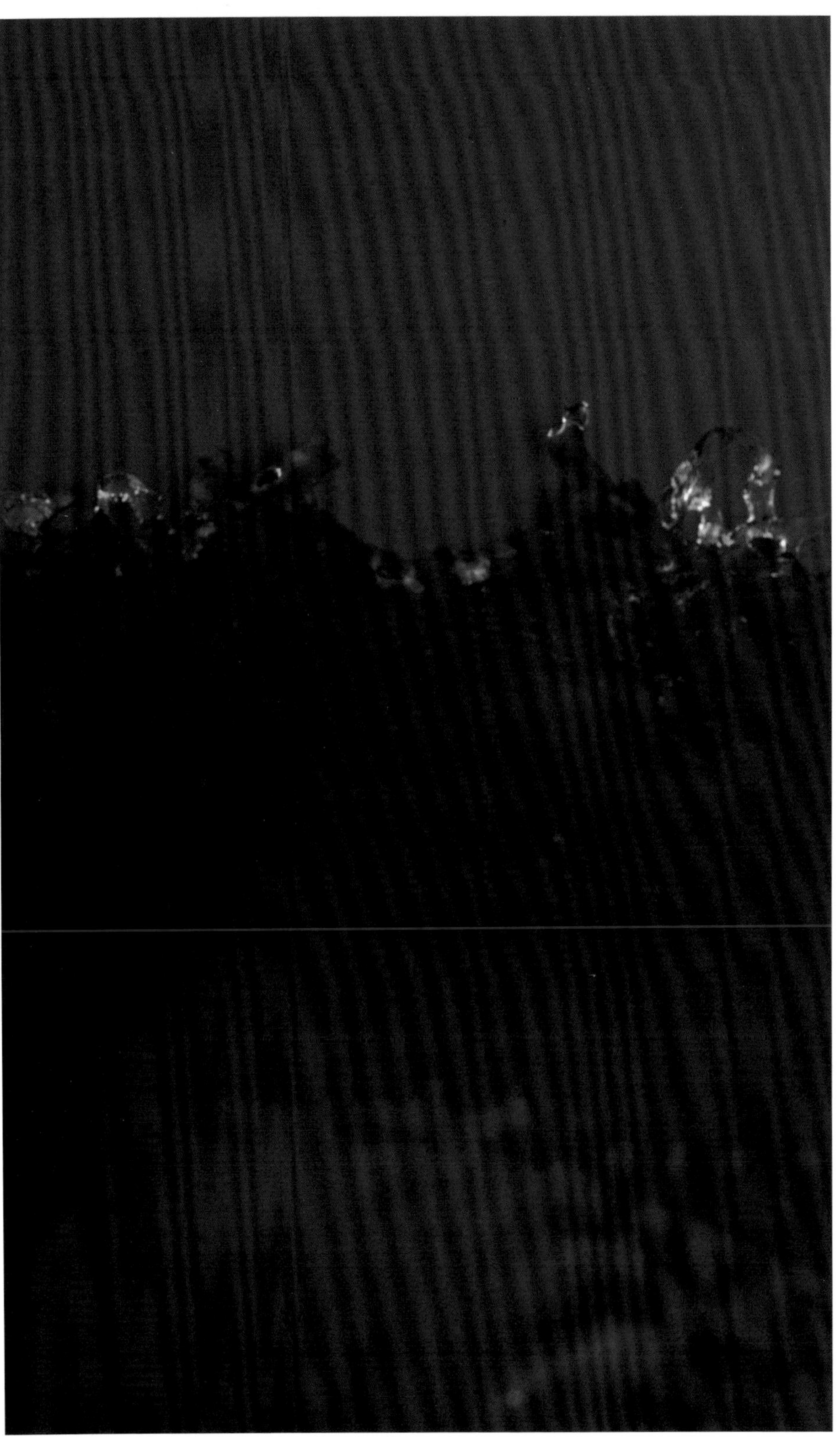

I switch, in conclusion, to my whisper, my sweet voice, my nighttime pillow voice, to say good-bye, adieu, auf Wiedersehen. I know that Shahryar and Sarah think I'm dead and gone. And I am. But in a way, I'm not … You'll see me again. Famous last words, right?

126

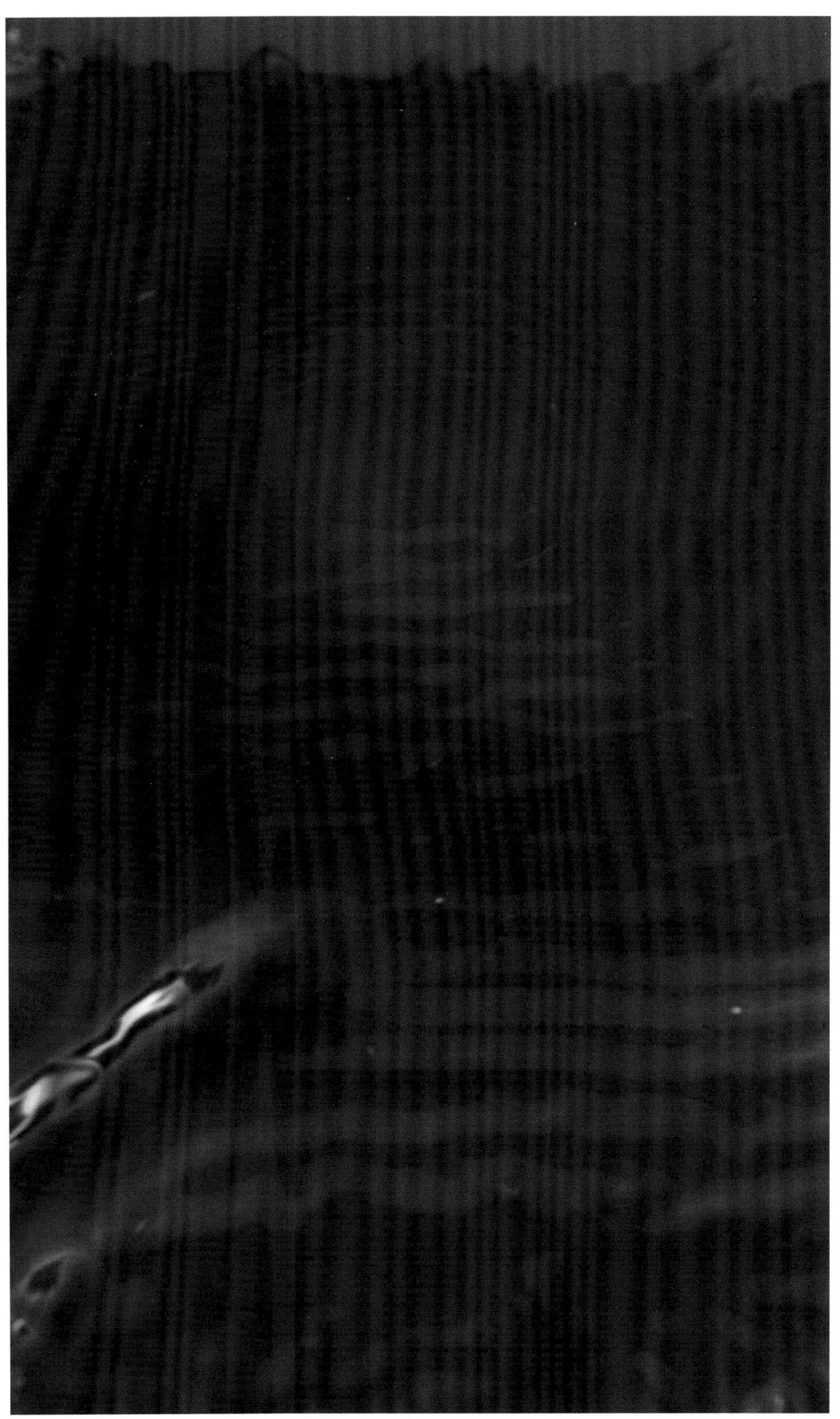

List of works

*Lounging Before a Staircase
Incident*, 2012 (detail)
Offset print and C-print on paper
100 × 70 cm and 50 × 44 cm, framed
Edition of 3 + 2 AP
Courtesy of Silberkuppe, Berlin   pp. 13/18

Factor Green, 2011
HD video, color, sound
6 min. 30 sec.
Stills
Edition of 5 + 2 AP
Courtesy of Rodeo Gallery, London,
and Silberkuppe, Berlin   pp. 14/15

Not the Stuff of Stone, 2011
Plaster, pigment, steel
62 × 135 × 35 cm
Julius Baer Art Collection, Zurich   p. 15

Replay the Ruse, 2012
HD video, color, sound
4 min. 45 sec.
Stills
Edition of 5 + 2 AP
Courtesy of Silberkuppe, Berlin,
and Rodeo Gallery, London   p. 16

Condition Report, 2012
Offset print and C-print on paper
100 × 70 cm and 50 × 44 cm, framed
Edition of 3 + 2 AP
Courtesy of Silberkuppe, Berlin   p. 18

Change of Events, 2012 (detail)
Offset print and C-print on paper
100 × 70 cm and 50 × 44 cm, framed
Edition of 3 + 2 AP
Courtesy of Silberkuppe, Berlin   p. 18

Parade, 2014
HD video, color, sound
38 min.
Stills
Edition of 5 + 2 AP
Courtesy of Rodeo Gallery, London,
and Silberkuppe, Berlin   p. 20

Hustle in Hand, 2014
HD video, color, sound
9 min. 40 sec.
Stills
Edition of 5 + 2 AP
Courtesy of Rodeo Gallery, London,
and Silberkuppe, Berlin   p. 20

Shahryar Nashat
Obituary

Text: Sarah Lehrer-Graiwer
CGI: Andrea Faraguna
Design: Aude Lehmann
Copyediting: Max Bach
Proofreading: Laura Preston
Color separations: Echelon, Santa Monica, CA
Printing: DZA Druckerei zu Altenburg, Germany

Acknowledgments:
Kirsty Bell, Alexandra Blättler,
Jörg Heiser, Christoph Keller,
Sylvia Kouvali, Isla Leaver-Yap,
Adam Linder, Luke Milne,
Aram Moshayedi, Sadegh Nashat,
Michael Turner, Gaëtan Varone,
Scott Cameron Weaver, Noura Wedell,
Rodeo Gallery, London, and
Silberkuppe, Berlin.

This publication is supported by:

Volkart Stiftung
Turnerstrasse 1
Postfach
CH-8401 Winterthur

Fonds d'art contemporain
Département de la culture et du sport
Rue des Bains 34
CH-1205 Geneva

SternbergPress

Caroline Schneider
Karl-Marx-Allee 78
D-10243 Berlin
www.sternberg-press.com

ISBN 978-3-95679-099-7

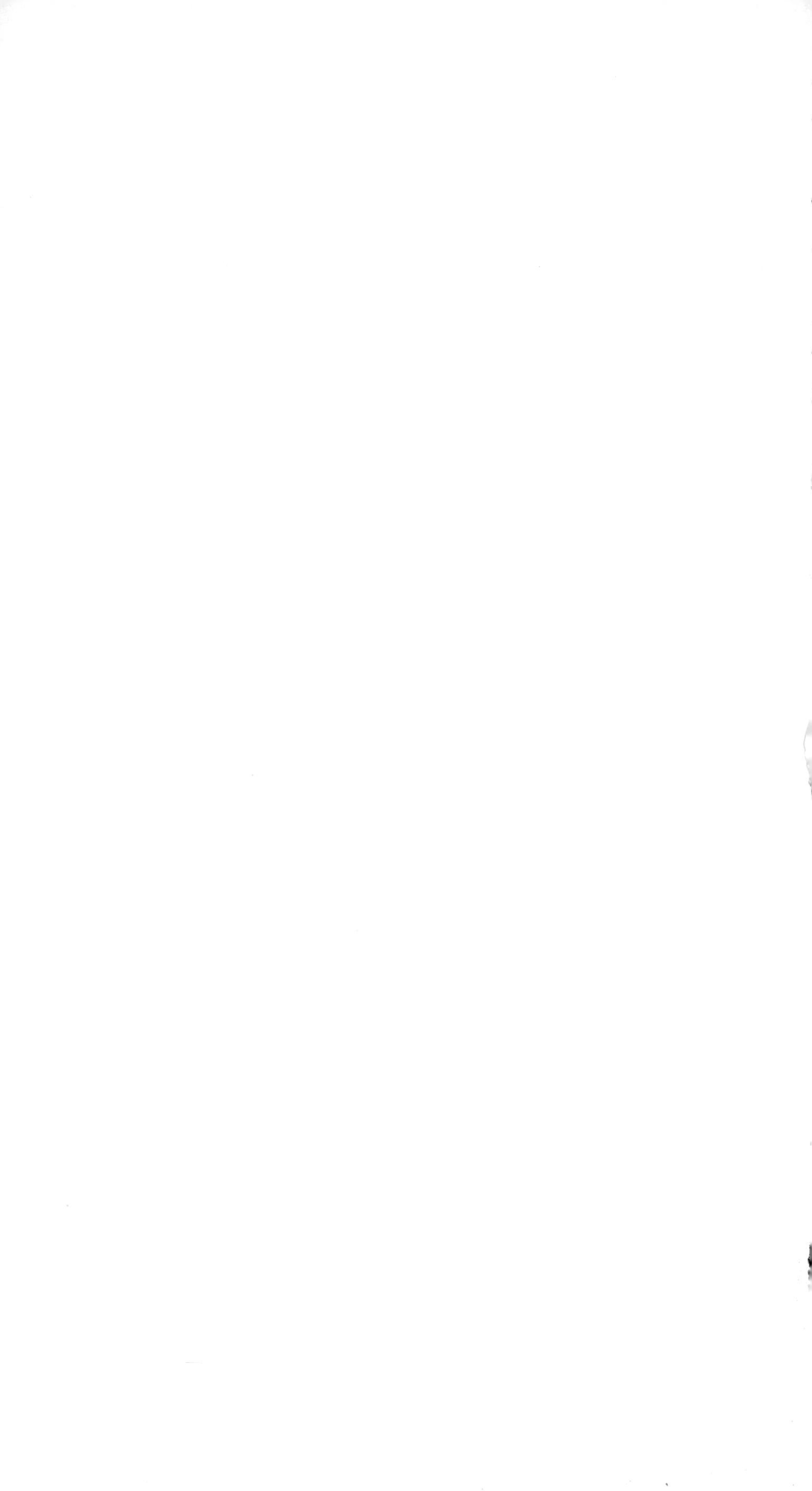